"After utilizing toolkits from The Art of Service, I was able to identify threats within my organization to which I was completely unaware. Using my team's knowledge as a competitive advantage, we now have superior systems that save time and energy."

"As a new Chief Technology Officer, I was feeling unprepared and inadequate to be successful in my role. I ordered an IT toolkit Sunday night and was prepared Monday morning to shed light on areas of improvement within my organization. I no longer felt overwhelmed and intimidated, I was excited to share what I had learned."

"I used the questionnaires to interview members of my team. I never knew how many insights we could produce collectively with our internal knowledge."

"I usually work until at least 8pm on weeknights. The Art of Service questionnaire saved me so much time and worry that Thursday night I attended my son's soccer game without sacrificing my professional obligations."

"After purchasing The Art of Service toolkit, I was able to identify areas where my company was not in compliance that could have put my job at risk. I looked like a hero when I proactively educated my team on the risks and presented a solid solution."

"I spent months shopping for an external consultant before realizing that The Art of Service would allow my team to consult themselves! Not only did we save time not catching a consultant up to speed, we were able to keep our company information and industry secrets confidential."

"Everyday there are new regulations and processes in my industry. The Art of Service toolkit has kept me ahead by using AI technology to constantly update the toolkits and address emerging needs."

"I customized The Art of Service toolkit to focus specifically on the concerns of my role and industry. I didn't have to waste time with a generic self-help book that wasn't tailored to my exact situation."

"Many of our competitors have asked us about our secret sauce. When I tell them it's the knowledge we have in-house, they never believe me. Little do they know The Art of Service toolkits are working behind the scenes."

"One of my friends hired a consultant who used the knowledge gained working with his company to advise their competitor. Talk about a competitive disadvantage! The Art of Service allowed us to keep our knowledge from walking out the door along with a huge portion of our budget in consulting fees."

"Honestly, I didn't know what I didn't know. Before purchasing The Art of Service, I didn't realize how many areas of my business needed to be refreshed and improved. I am so relieved The Art of Service was there to highlight our blind spots."

"Before The Art of Service, I waited eagerly for consulting company reports to come out each month. These reports kept us up to speed but provided little value because they put our competitors on the same playing field. With The Art of Service, we have uncovered unique insights to drive our business forward."

"Instead of investing extensive resources into an external consultant, we can spend more of our budget towards pursuing our company goals and objectives…while also spending a little more on corporate holiday parties."

"The risk of our competitors getting ahead has been mitigated because The Art of Service has provided us with a 360-degree view of threats within our organization before they even arise."

Microsoft Dynamics 365 For Finance And Operations Complete Self-Assessment Guide

Notice of rights

You are licensed to use the Self-Assessment contents in your presentations and materials for internal use and customers without asking us - we are here to help.

https://theartofservice.com
support@theartofservice.com

Table of Contents

About The Art of Service

The Art of Service, Business Process Architects since 2000, is dedicated to helping stakeholders achieve excellence.

Defining, designing, creating, and implementing a process to solve a stakeholders challenge or meet an objective is the most valuable role… In EVERY group, company, organization and department.

Unless you're talking a one-time, single-use project, there should be a process. Whether that process is managed and implemented by humans, AI, or a combination of the two, it needs to be designed by someone with a complex enough perspective to ask the right questions.

Someone capable of asking the right questions and step back and say, 'What are we really trying to accomplish here? And is there a different way to look at it?'

With The Art of Service's Self-Assessments, we empower people who can do just that — whether their title is marketer, entrepreneur, manager, salesperson, consultant, Business Process Manager, executive assistant, IT Manager, CIO etc... —they are the people who rule the future. They are people who watch the process as it happens, and ask the right questions to make the process work better.

Contact us when you need any support with this Self-Assessment and any help with templates, blue-prints and examples of standard documents you might need:

https://theartofservice.com
support@theartofservice.com

Included Resources - how to access

Included with your purchase of the book is the Microsoft

Dynamics 365 For Finance And Operations Self-Assessment Spreadsheet Dashboard which contains all questions and Self-Assessment areas and auto-generates insights, graphs, and project RACI planning - all with examples to get you started right away.

How? Simply send an email to
access@theartofservice.com
with this books' title in the subject to get the Microsoft Dynamics 365 For Finance And Operations Self Assessment Tool right away.

The auto reply will guide you further, you will then receive the following contents with New and Updated specific criteria:

- The latest quick edition of the book in PDF
- The latest complete edition of the book in PDF, which criteria correspond to the criteria in...
- The Self-Assessment Excel Dashboard, and...
- Example pre-filled Self-Assessment Excel Dashboard to get familiar with results generation
- In-depth specific Checklists covering the topic
- Project management checklists and templates to assist with implementation

INCLUDES LIFETIME SELF ASSESSMENT UPDATES

Every self assessment comes with Lifetime Updates and Lifetime Free Updated Books. Lifetime Updates is an industry-first feature which allows you to receive verified self assessment updates, ensuring you always have the most accurate information at your fingertips.

Get it now- you will be glad you did - do it now, before you forget.

Send an email to **access@theartofservice.com** with this books' title in the subject to get the Microsoft Dynamics 365 For Finance And Operations Self Assessment Tool right away.

Purpose of this Self-Assessment

This Self-Assessment has been developed to improve understanding of the requirements and elements of Microsoft Dynamics 365 For Finance And Operations, based on best practices and standards in business process architecture, design and quality management.

It is designed to allow for a rapid Self-Assessment to determine how closely existing management practices and procedures correspond to the elements of the Self-Assessment.

The criteria of requirements and elements of Microsoft Dynamics 365 For Finance And Operations have been rephrased in the format of a Self-Assessment questionnaire, with a seven-criterion scoring system, as explained in this document.

In this format, even with limited background knowledge of Microsoft Dynamics 365 For Finance And Operations, a manager can quickly review existing operations to determine how they measure up to the standards. This in turn can serve as the starting point of a 'gap analysis' to identify management tools or system elements that might usefully be implemented in the organization to help improve overall performance.

How to use the Self-Assessment

On the following pages are a series of questions to identify to what extent your Microsoft Dynamics 365 For Finance And Operations initiative is complete in comparison to the requirements set in standards.

To facilitate answering the questions, there is a space in front of each question to enter a score on a scale of '1' to '5'.

1 Strongly Disagree

2 Disagree

3 Neutral

4 Agree

5 Strongly Agree

Read the question and rate it with the following in front of mind:

'In my belief, the answer to this question is clearly defined'.

There are two ways in which you can choose to interpret this statement;

1. how aware are you that the answer to the question is clearly defined
2. for more in-depth analysis you can choose to gather evidence and confirm the answer to the question. This obviously will take more time, most Self-Assessment users opt for the first way to interpret the question

and dig deeper later on based on the outcome of the overall Self-Assessment.

A score of '1' would mean that the answer is not clear at all, where a '5' would mean the answer is crystal clear and defined. Leave emtpy when the question is not applicable or you don't want to answer it, you can skip it without affecting your score. Write your score in the space provided.

After you have responded to all the appropriate statements in each section, compute your average score for that section, using the formula provided, and round to the nearest tenth. Then transfer to the corresponding spoke in the Microsoft Dynamics 365 For Finance And Operations Scorecard on the second next page of the Self-Assessment.

Your completed Microsoft Dynamics 365 For Finance And Operations Scorecard will give you a clear presentation of which Microsoft Dynamics 365 For Finance And Operations areas need attention.

Microsoft Dynamics 365 For Finance And Operations Scorecard Example

Example of how the finalized Scorecard can look like:

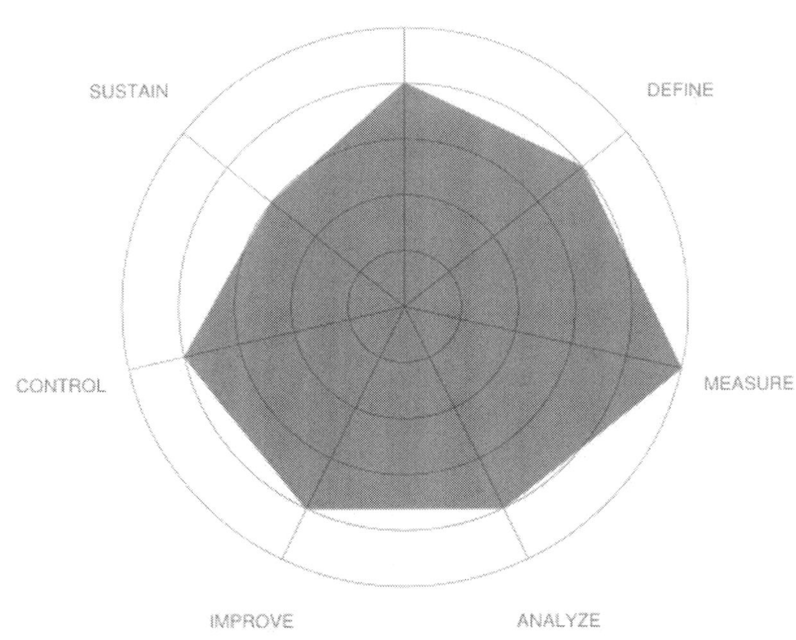

Microsoft Dynamics 365 For Finance And Operations Scorecard

Your Scores:

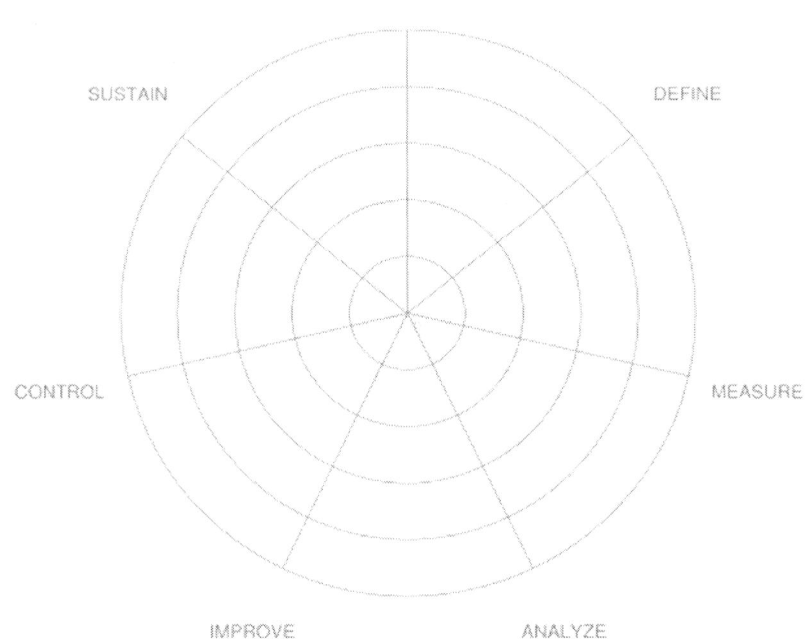

BEGINNING OF THE SELF-ASSESSMENT:

CRITERION #1: RECOGNIZE

INTENT: Be aware of the need for change. Recognize that there is an unfavorable variation, problem or symptom.

In my belief, the answer to this question is clearly defined:

5 Strongly Agree

4 Agree

3 Neutral

2 Disagree

1 Strongly Disagree

1. How are the Microsoft Dynamics 365 for Finance and Operations's objectives aligned to the group's overall stakeholder strategy?
<--- Score

2. Are there recognized Microsoft Dynamics 365 for Finance and Operations problems?
<--- Score

3. Does your organizations current IT staff have the appropriate skill set needed to support future organization technologies?
<--- Score

4. How many file servers should you identify?
<--- Score

5. Are controls defined to recognize and contain problems?
<--- Score

6. How often do you experience problems with the timeliness of service completion?
<--- Score

7. What do you need to start doing?
<--- Score

8. Do you recognize Microsoft Dynamics 365 for Finance and Operations achievements?
<--- Score

9. Do your communications need a consistent look?
<--- Score

10. Why the need?
<--- Score

11. Do you need to revisit and clarify your values?
<--- Score

12. What is the problem and/or vulnerability?
<--- Score

13. Who are your key stakeholders who need to sign off?
<--- Score

14. How does the finance function need to change to enable business agility?
<--- Score

15. What is the problem or issue?
<--- Score

16. Do you use the scheduler for things beyond field service/project service needs?
<--- Score

17. Is there a mobile App for the Event Management?
<--- Score

18. What problems are you facing and how do you consider Microsoft Dynamics 365 for Finance and Operations will circumvent those obstacles?
<--- Score

19. Are there Microsoft Dynamics 365 for Finance and Operations problems defined?
<--- Score

20. What prevents you from making the changes you know will make you a more effective Microsoft Dynamics 365 for Finance and Operations leader?
<--- Score

21. Are problem definition and motivation clearly presented?
<--- Score

22. What situation(s) led to this Microsoft Dynamics 365 for Finance and Operations Self Assessment?
<--- Score

23. What Microsoft Dynamics 365 for Finance and Operations coordination do you need?
<--- Score

24. Are you dealing with any of the same issues today as yesterday? What can you do about this?
<--- Score

25. Who should resolve the Microsoft Dynamics 365 for Finance and Operations issues?
<--- Score

26. For your Microsoft Dynamics 365 for Finance and Operations project, identify and describe the business environment, is there more than one layer to the business environment?
<--- Score

27. Would you recognize a threat from the inside?
<--- Score

28. What needs to stay?
<--- Score

29. Do you need different Dynamics 365 licenses to deploy to Azure?
<--- Score

30. How much are sponsors, customers, partners, stakeholders involved in Microsoft Dynamics 365 for Finance and Operations? In other words, what are

the risks, if Microsoft Dynamics 365 for Finance and Operations does not deliver successfully?
<--- Score

31. Whom do you really need or want to serve?
<--- Score

32. Will it solve real problems?
<--- Score

33. What are the clients issues and concerns?
<--- Score

34. What is the Microsoft Dynamics 365 for Finance and Operations problem definition? What do you need to resolve?
<--- Score

35. Do you need different information or graphics?
<--- Score

36. How can auditing be a preventative security measure?
<--- Score

37. Where is training needed?
<--- Score

38. What is the extent or complexity of the Microsoft Dynamics 365 for Finance and Operations problem?
<--- Score

39. Is there a minimum amount of users that you need?
<--- Score

40. Is event management part of Microsoft Dynamics portal or something else?
<--- Score

41. Which needs are not included or involved?
<--- Score

42. To what extent does each concerned units management team recognize Microsoft Dynamics 365 for Finance and Operations as an effective investment?
<--- Score

43. Do you need to avoid or amend any Microsoft Dynamics 365 for Finance and Operations activities?
<--- Score

44. Are there any specific expectations or concerns about the Microsoft Dynamics 365 for Finance and Operations team, Microsoft Dynamics 365 for Finance and Operations itself?
<--- Score

45. Is the quality assurance team identified?
<--- Score

46. What are the expected benefits of Microsoft Dynamics 365 for Finance and Operations to the stakeholder?
<--- Score

47. How does it fit into your organizational needs and tasks?
<--- Score

48. What should be considered when identifying

available resources, constraints, and deadlines?
<--- Score

49. What do you need to know to deploy Dynamics 365 on Azure?
<--- Score

50. Did you miss any major Microsoft Dynamics 365 for Finance and Operations issues?
<--- Score

51. What would happen if Microsoft Dynamics 365 for Finance and Operations weren't done?
<--- Score

52. What does Microsoft Dynamics 365 for Finance and Operations success mean to the stakeholders?
<--- Score

53. Who defines the rules in relation to any given issue?
<--- Score

54. What are the stakeholder objectives to be achieved with Microsoft Dynamics 365 for Finance and Operations?
<--- Score

55. Do you need to add or upgrade any clients?
<--- Score

56. Do you have compatibility problems with other systems?
<--- Score

57. Are you in need of a top producing sales

professional?
<--- Score

58. Consider your own Microsoft Dynamics 365 for Finance and Operations project, what types of organizational problems do you think might be causing or affecting your problem, based on the work done so far?
<--- Score

59. As a sponsor, customer or management, how important is it to meet goals, objectives?
<--- Score

60. What new software or tools will your users need?
<--- Score

61. What if a customer needs an additional Marketing application?
<--- Score

62. How are you going to measure success?
<--- Score

63. Which servers should you identify?
<--- Score

64. Where do you need to exercise leadership?
<--- Score

65. Who needs budgets?
<--- Score

66. Who else hopes to benefit from it?
<--- Score

67. What about multi-user registration, e.g. need to register my staff?
<--- Score

68. When a Microsoft Dynamics 365 for Finance and Operations manager recognizes a problem, what options are available?
<--- Score

69. What information do users need?
<--- Score

70. What about your internal stakeholders – your members – needs?
<--- Score

71. How are training requirements identified?
<--- Score

72. Are employees recognized for desired behaviors?
<--- Score

73. Do you have/need 24-hour access to key personnel?
<--- Score

74. What do employees need in the short term?
<--- Score

Add up total points for this section:
_____ = Total points for this section

Divided by: ______ (number of statements answered) = ______
Average score for this section

Transfer your score to the Microsoft Dynamics 365 for Finance and Operations Index at the beginning of the Self-Assessment.

CRITERION #2: DEFINE:

INTENT: Formulate the stakeholder problem. Define the problem, needs and objectives.

In my belief, the answer to this question is clearly defined:

5 Strongly Agree

4 Agree

3 Neutral

2 Disagree

1 Strongly Disagree

1. What specifically is the problem? Where does it occur? When does it occur? What is its extent?
<--- Score

2. Is there a Microsoft Dynamics 365 for Finance and Operations management charter, including stakeholder case, problem and goal statements, scope, milestones, roles and responsibilities, communication plan?

<--- Score

3. Has the improvement team collected the 'voice of the customer' (obtained feedback – qualitative and quantitative)?
<--- Score

4. Is scope creep really all bad news?
<--- Score

5. Is server side sync a requirement for auto capture?
<--- Score

6. What is out of scope?
<--- Score

7. Is a fully trained team formed, supported, and committed to work on the Microsoft Dynamics 365 for Finance and Operations improvements?
<--- Score

8. How do you hand over Microsoft Dynamics 365 for Finance and Operations context?
<--- Score

9. Is the current 'as is' process being followed? If not, what are the discrepancies?
<--- Score

10. Are stakeholder processes mapped?
<--- Score

11. What are your hardware and software requirements?
<--- Score

12. Who are the Microsoft Dynamics 365 for Finance and Operations improvement team members, including Management Leads and Coaches?
<--- Score

13. Is the team sponsored by a champion or stakeholder leader?
<--- Score

14. What background or experience is required or helpful?
<--- Score

15. How do you manage scope?
<--- Score

16. What customer feedback methods were used to solicit their input?
<--- Score

17. What is the definition of Microsoft Dynamics 365 for Finance and Operations excellence?
<--- Score

18. Is the scope of Microsoft Dynamics 365 for Finance and Operations defined?
<--- Score

19. Do some work groups require customized configuration settings?
<--- Score

20. Is full participation by members in regularly held team meetings guaranteed?
<--- Score

21. What knowledge or experience is required?
<--- Score

22. What scope to assess?
<--- Score

23. Is the team equipped with available and reliable resources?
<--- Score

24. Is the Microsoft Dynamics 365 for Finance and Operations scope manageable?
<--- Score

25. How and when will the baselines be defined?
<--- Score

26. How is the team tracking and documenting its work?
<--- Score

27. Is Microsoft Dynamics 365 for Finance and Operations currently on schedule according to the plan?
<--- Score

28. What intelligence can you gather?
<--- Score

29. Do customer engagement licenses count towards unified operations minimum purchase requirements?
<--- Score

30. How do you catch Microsoft Dynamics 365 for

Finance and Operations definition inconsistencies?
<--- Score

31. What are the rough order estimates on cost savings/opportunities that Microsoft Dynamics 365 for Finance and Operations brings?
<--- Score

32. What critical content must be communicated – who, what, when, where, and how?
<--- Score

33. What requirements must be known before the determination is made to move to the cloud?
<--- Score

34. Is data collected and displayed to better understand customer(s) critical needs and requirements.
<--- Score

35. What key stakeholder process output measure(s) does Microsoft Dynamics 365 for Finance and Operations leverage and how?
<--- Score

36. What would be the goal or target for a Microsoft Dynamics 365 for Finance and Operations's improvement team?
<--- Score

37. Are resources adequate for the scope?
<--- Score

38. Has a team charter been developed and communicated?

<--- Score

39. When is/was the Microsoft Dynamics 365 for Finance and Operations start date?
<--- Score

40. What is the service teams average case duration?
<--- Score

41. How does the Microsoft Dynamics 365 for Finance and Operations manager ensure against scope creep?
<--- Score

42. What are the Microsoft Dynamics 365 for Finance and Operations use cases?
<--- Score

43. What are the compelling stakeholder reasons for embarking on Microsoft Dynamics 365 for Finance and Operations?
<--- Score

44. How are consistent Microsoft Dynamics 365 for Finance and Operations definitions important?
<--- Score

45. Is the team formed and are team leaders (Coaches and Management Leads) assigned?
<--- Score

46. What constraints exist that might impact the team?
<--- Score

47. What Microsoft Dynamics 365 for Finance and

Operations requirements should be gathered?
<--- Score

48. When is the estimated completion date?
<--- Score

49. What happens if Microsoft Dynamics 365 for Finance and Operations's scope changes?
<--- Score

50. Has anyone else (internal or external to the group) attempted to solve this problem or a similar one before? If so, what knowledge can be leveraged from these previous efforts?
<--- Score

51. Are roles and responsibilities formally defined?
<--- Score

52. What is the scope of the Microsoft Dynamics 365 for Finance and Operations effort?
<--- Score

53. Are the Microsoft Dynamics 365 for Finance and Operations requirements testable?
<--- Score

54. Do new requirements apply to FTE only or subcontractors?
<--- Score

55. Is the team adequately staffed with the desired cross-functionality? If not, what additional resources are available to the team?
<--- Score

56. What is the scope of the project?
<--- Score

57. Do you also offer test case chains that can be used to perform regression tests or user acceptance tests directly?
<--- Score

58. Are there any constraints known that bear on the ability to perform Microsoft Dynamics 365 for Finance and Operations work? How is the team addressing them?
<--- Score

59. What is the definition of success?
<--- Score

60. Are improvement team members fully trained on Microsoft Dynamics 365 for Finance and Operations?
<--- Score

61. How do you manage unclear Microsoft Dynamics 365 for Finance and Operations requirements?
<--- Score

62. Has the Microsoft Dynamics 365 for Finance and Operations work been fairly and/or equitably divided and delegated among team members who are qualified and capable to perform the work? Has everyone contributed?
<--- Score

63. Has the current organization of record been commissioned to complete the current scope of website work?
<--- Score

64. Has a Microsoft Dynamics 365 for Finance and Operations requirement not been met?
<--- Score

65. Has everyone on the team, including the team leaders, been properly trained?
<--- Score

66. Where can you gather more information?
<--- Score

67. Is there a completed SIPOC representation, describing the Suppliers, Inputs, Process, Outputs, and Customers?
<--- Score

68. How was the 'as is' process map developed, reviewed, verified and validated?
<--- Score

69. What are the dynamics of the communication plan?
<--- Score

70. Who is gathering Microsoft Dynamics 365 for Finance and Operations information?
<--- Score

71. Are different versions of process maps needed to account for the different types of inputs?
<--- Score

72. What are the boundaries of the scope? What is in bounds and what is not? What is the start point? What is the stop point?

<--- Score

73. What are the tasks and definitions?
<--- Score

74. What Microsoft Dynamics 365 for Finance and Operations services do you require?
<--- Score

75. Is there any additional Microsoft Dynamics 365 for Finance and Operations definition of success?
<--- Score

76. Is the Microsoft Dynamics 365 for Finance and Operations scope complete and appropriately sized?
<--- Score

77. In what way can you redefine the criteria of choice clients have in your category in your favor?
<--- Score

78. What was the context?
<--- Score

79. Is there a minimum user requirement?
<--- Score

80. Does the scope remain the same?
<--- Score

81. If substitutes have been appointed, have they been briefed on the Microsoft Dynamics 365 for Finance and Operations goals and received regular communications as to the progress to date?
<--- Score

82. Will team members regularly document their Microsoft Dynamics 365 for Finance and Operations work?
<--- Score

83. Are team charters developed?
<--- Score

84. Has/have the customer(s) been identified?
<--- Score

85. What baselines are required to be defined and managed?
<--- Score

86. Are the Microsoft Dynamics 365 for Finance and Operations requirements complete?
<--- Score

87. Will team members perform Microsoft Dynamics 365 for Finance and Operations work when assigned and in a timely fashion?
<--- Score

88. Is Microsoft Dynamics 365 for Finance and Operations linked to key stakeholder goals and objectives?
<--- Score

89. Does the team have regular meetings?
<--- Score

90. What must your organization associate require of its vendors?
<--- Score

91. Is special Microsoft Dynamics 365 for Finance and Operations user knowledge required?
<--- Score

92. Is the work to date meeting requirements?
<--- Score

93. How will the Microsoft Dynamics 365 for Finance and Operations team and the group measure complete success of Microsoft Dynamics 365 for Finance and Operations?
<--- Score

94. Has a high-level 'as is' process map been completed, verified and validated?
<--- Score

95. Is there regularly 100% attendance at the team meetings? If not, have appointed substitutes attended to preserve cross-functionality and full representation?
<--- Score

96. Do you have organizational privacy requirements?
<--- Score

97. Who is gathering information?
<--- Score

98. What gets examined?
<--- Score

99. Are there different segments of customers?
<--- Score

100. What are the Roles and Responsibilities for

each team member and its leadership? Where is this documented?
<--- Score

101. Do corresponding new requirements apply to FTE only or subcontractors?
<--- Score

102. Is the improvement team aware of the different versions of a process: what they think it is vs. what it actually is vs. what it should be vs. what it could be?
<--- Score

103. How do you build the right business case?
<--- Score

104. What information do you gather?
<--- Score

105. Have the customer needs been translated into specific, measurable requirements? How?
<--- Score

106. Is there a completed, verified, and validated high-level 'as is' (not 'should be' or 'could be') stakeholder process map?
<--- Score

107. Are required metrics defined, what are they?
<--- Score

108. Are customer(s) identified and segmented according to their different needs and requirements?
<--- Score

109. Are audit criteria, scope, frequency and methods

defined?
<--- Score

110. Has the direction changed at all during the course of Microsoft Dynamics 365 for Finance and Operations? If so, when did it change and why?
<--- Score

111. Is it clearly defined in and to your organization what you do?
<--- Score

112. Who approved the Microsoft Dynamics 365 for Finance and Operations scope?
<--- Score

113. Are customers identified and high impact areas defined?
<--- Score

114. Why are you doing Microsoft Dynamics 365 for Finance and Operations and what is the scope?
<--- Score

115. How do you keep key subject matter experts in the loop?
<--- Score

116. What should do on the child form to ensure the business requirements are fulfilled?
<--- Score

117. When are meeting minutes sent out? Who is on the distribution list?
<--- Score

118. Is there a clear Microsoft Dynamics 365 for Finance and Operations case definition?
<--- Score

119. How did the Microsoft Dynamics 365 for Finance and Operations manager receive input to the development of a Microsoft Dynamics 365 for Finance and Operations improvement plan and the estimated completion dates/times of each activity?
<--- Score

120. Do the problem and goal statements meet the SMART criteria (specific, measurable, attainable, relevant, and time-bound)?
<--- Score

121. How would you define Microsoft Dynamics 365 for Finance and Operations leadership?
<--- Score

122. What defines best in class?
<--- Score

123. Do you have a Microsoft Dynamics 365 for Finance and Operations success story or case study ready to tell and share?
<--- Score

124. How often are the team meetings?
<--- Score

125. How will variation in the actual durations of each activity be dealt with to ensure that the expected Microsoft Dynamics 365 for Finance and Operations results are met?
<--- Score

126. Have all of the relationships been defined properly?
<--- Score

127. Are task requirements clearly defined?
<--- Score

128. Who defines (or who defined) the rules and roles?
<--- Score

129. Has a project plan, Gantt chart, or similar been developed/completed?
<--- Score

130. How do you gather requirements?
<--- Score

131. Is there a critical path to deliver Microsoft Dynamics 365 for Finance and Operations results?
<--- Score

Add up total points for this section:
_____ = Total points for this section

Divided by: ______ (number of statements answered) = ______ Average score for this section

Transfer your score to the Microsoft Dynamics 365 for Finance and Operations Index at the beginning of the Self-Assessment.

CRITERION #3: MEASURE:

INTENT: Gather the correct data. Measure the current performance and evolution of the situation.

In my belief, the answer to this question is clearly defined:

5 Strongly Agree

4 Agree

3 Neutral

2 Disagree

1 Strongly Disagree

1. How are measurements made?
<--- Score

2. When are costs are incurred?
<--- Score

3. What would it cost to replace your technology?
<--- Score

4. What are the key input variables? What are the key process variables? What are the key output variables?
<--- Score

5. How do the Additional Database Storage changes impact existing customers?
<--- Score

6. How will effects be measured?
<--- Score

7. Is data collected on key measures that were identified?
<--- Score

8. Are there precautions that you should take when acquiring samples for organization analysis?
<--- Score

9. What data was collected (past, present, future/ongoing)?
<--- Score

10. Does Microsoft Dynamics 365 for Finance and Operations systematically track and analyze outcomes for accountability and quality improvement?
<--- Score

11. Does Microsoft Dynamics 365 for Finance and Operations analysis isolate the fundamental causes of problems?
<--- Score

12. How can you measure the performance?
<--- Score

13. What is the right balance of time and resources between investigation, analysis, and discussion and dissemination?
<--- Score

14. Who is involved in verifying compliance?
<--- Score

15. Has a cost center been established?
<--- Score

16. Did you tackle the cause or the symptom?
<--- Score

17. How is progress measured?
<--- Score

18. Was a data collection plan established?
<--- Score

19. Can you measure the return on analysis?
<--- Score

20. How do your measurements capture actionable Microsoft Dynamics 365 for Finance and Operations information for use in exceeding your customers expectations and securing your customers engagement?
<--- Score

21. How can you manage cost down?
<--- Score

22. Is there a Performance Baseline?
<--- Score

23. Is data collection planned and executed?
<--- Score

24. What is the Microsoft Dynamics 365 for Finance and Operations business impact?
<--- Score

25. Is there industry focus being put on the development of the sales app?
<--- Score

26. Have you made assumptions about the shape of the future, particularly its impact on your customers and competitors?
<--- Score

27. Which Microsoft Dynamics 365 for Finance and Operations impacts are significant?
<--- Score

28. What are the costs of delaying Microsoft Dynamics 365 for Finance and Operations action?
<--- Score

29. How will measures be used to manage and adapt?
<--- Score

30. Are the measurements objective?
<--- Score

31. Are high impact defects defined and identified in the stakeholder process?
<--- Score

32. Are there any easy-to-implement alternatives to Microsoft Dynamics 365 for Finance and Operations?

Sometimes other solutions are available that do not require the cost implications of a full-blown project?
<--- Score

33. How do you aggregate measures across priorities?
<--- Score

34. Does your organization systematically track and analyze outcomes related for accountability and quality improvement?
<--- Score

35. How large is the gap between current performance and the customer-specified (goal) performance?
<--- Score

36. How do you quantify and qualify impacts?
<--- Score

37. What do people want to verify?
<--- Score

38. Are losses documented, analyzed, and remedial processes developed to prevent future losses?
<--- Score

39. What has the team done to assure the stability and accuracy of the measurement process?
<--- Score

40. Does a Microsoft Dynamics 365 for Finance and Operations quantification method exist?
<--- Score

41. Is the cost worth the Microsoft Dynamics 365 for

Finance and Operations effort ?
<--- Score

42. How do you know that any Microsoft Dynamics 365 for Finance and Operations analysis is complete and comprehensive?
<--- Score

43. How will your organization measure success?
<--- Score

44. What do you measure and why?
<--- Score

45. How will you measure your Microsoft Dynamics 365 for Finance and Operations effectiveness?
<--- Score

46. Is key measure data collection planned and executed, process variation displayed and communicated and performance baselined?
<--- Score

47. What is the total fixed cost?
<--- Score

48. What are the current costs of the Microsoft Dynamics 365 for Finance and Operations process?
<--- Score

49. Are the Microsoft Dynamics 365 for Finance and Operations benefits worth its costs?
<--- Score

50. Have all non-recommended alternatives been analyzed in sufficient detail?

<--- Score

51. How will the Microsoft Dynamics 365 for Finance and Operations data be analyzed?
<--- Score

52. Have the types of risks that may impact Microsoft Dynamics 365 for Finance and Operations been identified and analyzed?
<--- Score

53. How do you stay flexible and focused to recognize larger Microsoft Dynamics 365 for Finance and Operations results?
<--- Score

54. Is the chart and dashboard only for the partner portal or do you use in other portals as customer, custom, or others?
<--- Score

55. Are process variation components displayed/ communicated using suitable charts, graphs, plots?
<--- Score

56. What is your cost benefit analysis?
<--- Score

57. What users will be impacted?
<--- Score

58. What key measures identified indicate the performance of the stakeholder process?
<--- Score

59. Does Microsoft Dynamics 365 for Finance and

Operations analysis show the relationships among important Microsoft Dynamics 365 for Finance and Operations factors?
<--- Score

60. Who should receive measurement reports?
<--- Score

61. What costs and benefits emerge from quality management?
<--- Score

62. What charts has the team used to display the components of variation in the process?
<--- Score

63. Have the concerns of stakeholders to help identify and define potential barriers been obtained and analyzed?
<--- Score

64. Does a workflow approval adversely impact the timing of a process?
<--- Score

65. How do you measure efficient delivery of Microsoft Dynamics 365 for Finance and Operations services?
<--- Score

66. Are there measurements based on task performance?
<--- Score

67. Has reporting become costly for your organization?

<--- Score

68. Are missed Microsoft Dynamics 365 for Finance and Operations opportunities costing your organization money?
<--- Score

69. Are key measures identified and agreed upon?
<--- Score

70. What are your customers expectations and measures?
<--- Score

71. Is it possible to estimate the impact of unanticipated complexity such as wrong or failed assumptions, feedback, etcetera on proposed reforms?
<--- Score

72. Why do the measurements/indicators matter?
<--- Score

73. Does management have the right priorities among projects?
<--- Score

74. Has a cost benefit analysis been performed?
<--- Score

75. Do you have an issue in getting priority?
<--- Score

76. How frequently do you track Microsoft Dynamics 365 for Finance and Operations measures?
<--- Score

77. What is measured? Why?
<--- Score

78. What are the estimated costs of proposed changes?
<--- Score

79. What does your operating model cost?
<--- Score

80. How long to keep data and how to manage retention costs?
<--- Score

81. Have changes been properly/adequately analyzed for effect?
<--- Score

82. How can you reduce the costs of obtaining inputs?
<--- Score

83. Is your workforce centralised enough to make a traditional work environment viable – and cost effective?
<--- Score

84. What are your operating costs?
<--- Score

85. What could cause delays in the schedule?
<--- Score

86. Where can you go to verify the info?
<--- Score

87. What is your Microsoft Dynamics 365 for Finance and Operations quality cost segregation study?
<--- Score

88. How do you verify Microsoft Dynamics 365 for Finance and Operations completeness and accuracy?
<--- Score

89. What could cause you to change course?
<--- Score

90. Who participated in the data collection for measurements?
<--- Score

91. Among the Microsoft Dynamics 365 for Finance and Operations product and service cost to be estimated, which is considered hardest to estimate?
<--- Score

92. Is there an opportunity to verify requirements?
<--- Score

93. What exactly is cloud computing, and how does it impact the work of risk managers?
<--- Score

94. Is the project add in include license cost?
<--- Score

95. Are you able to realize any cost savings?
<--- Score

96. Is a follow-up focused external Microsoft Dynamics 365 for Finance and Operations review required?

<--- Score

97. What are your primary costs, revenues, assets?
<--- Score

98. What is the cost of rework?
<--- Score

99. What evidence is there and what is measured?
<--- Score

100. How complex are your current analysis and how frequently do you currently process data?
<--- Score

101. At what cost?
<--- Score

102. What are the strategic priorities for this year?
<--- Score

103. How will changes impact customization?
<--- Score

104. How much will Dynamics 365 cost?
<--- Score

105. Is the impact of blockchain technology taken into account?
<--- Score

106. What does verifying compliance entail?
<--- Score

107. How do you leverage the full potential of your data to obtain greater insight, control, and

impact?
<--- Score

108. Are there specific requirements on the email recipient side to make sure you can get the analytics?
<--- Score

109. What are the costs and benefits?
<--- Score

110. What are hidden Microsoft Dynamics 365 for Finance and Operations quality costs?
<--- Score

111. What are you primary metrics for internal quality measurement regarding timeliness?
<--- Score

112. How do you measure variability?
<--- Score

113. Is Process Variation Displayed/Communicated?
<--- Score

114. Is long term and short term variability accounted for?
<--- Score

115. How do you verify the authenticity of the data and information used?
<--- Score

116. What causes mismanagement?
<--- Score

117. Do the benefits outweigh the costs?
<--- Score

118. Is a solid data collection plan established that includes measurement systems analysis?
<--- Score

119. Is the project considered to be a priority?
<--- Score

120. What are your key Microsoft Dynamics 365 for Finance and Operations indicators that you will measure, analyze and track?
<--- Score

121. Will Microsoft Dynamics 365 for Finance and Operations have an impact on current business continuity, disaster recovery processes and/or infrastructure?
<--- Score

122. Have you found any 'ground fruit' or 'low-hanging fruit' for immediate remedies to the gap in performance?
<--- Score

123. Have you included everything in your Microsoft Dynamics 365 for Finance and Operations cost models?
<--- Score

124. What methods are feasible and acceptable to estimate the impact of reforms?
<--- Score

125. Do you verify that corrective actions were taken?

<--- Score

126. What are the agreed upon definitions of the high impact areas, defect(s), unit(s), and opportunities that will figure into the process capability metrics?
<--- Score

127. How sensitive must the Microsoft Dynamics 365 for Finance and Operations strategy be to cost?
<--- Score

128. Was a Microsoft Dynamics 365 for Finance and Operations charter developed?
<--- Score

129. How do you take advantage of low cost, highly available cloud services?
<--- Score

130. What are the Microsoft Dynamics 365 for Finance and Operations key cost drivers?
<--- Score

131. Which measures and indicators matter?
<--- Score

132. What particular quality tools did the team find helpful in establishing measurements?
<--- Score

133. What are predictive Microsoft Dynamics 365 for Finance and Operations analytics?
<--- Score

134. How complex are your current analyses and how frequently do you currently process data?

<--- Score

135. What analytical skills are you interested in expanding or willing to expand to?
<--- Score

136. What are the operational costs after Microsoft Dynamics 365 for Finance and Operations deployment?
<--- Score

137. What are the costs?
<--- Score

138. Are you taking your company in the direction of better and revenue or cheaper and cost?
<--- Score

139. How is performance measured?
<--- Score

Add up total points for this section:
_____ = Total points for this section

Divided by: ______ (number of statements answered) = ______ Average score for this section

Transfer your score to the Microsoft Dynamics 365 for Finance and Operations Index at the beginning of the Self-Assessment.

CRITERION #4: ANALYZE:

INTENT: Analyze causes, assumptions and hypotheses.

In my belief, the answer to this question is clearly defined:

5 Strongly Agree

4 Agree

3 Neutral

2 Disagree

1 Strongly Disagree

1. How is the data gathered?
<--- Score

2. What customer needs drive requirements and what are the current limitations?
<--- Score

3. How modified is your data schema?
<--- Score

4. Was a cause-and-effect diagram used to explore the different types of causes (or sources of variation)?
<--- Score

5. What is the general process of upgrading your system to Dynamics 365?
<--- Score

6. What are the disruptive Microsoft Dynamics 365 for Finance and Operations technologies that enable your organization to radically change your business processes?
<--- Score

7. What quality tools were used to get through the analyze phase?
<--- Score

8. What are the processes for audit reporting and management?
<--- Score

9. Are you missing Microsoft Dynamics 365 for Finance and Operations opportunities?
<--- Score

10. Were Pareto charts (or similar) used to portray the 'heavy hitters' (or key sources of variation)?
<--- Score

11. What data do you need to collect?
<--- Score

12. What is the complexity of the output produced?
<--- Score

13. Are gaps between current performance and the goal performance identified?
<--- Score

14. How much time is required for a test case to be completed with your data and how long does the test itself take?
<--- Score

15. What Microsoft Dynamics 365 for Finance and Operations data do you gather or use now?
<--- Score

16. How has the Microsoft Dynamics 365 for Finance and Operations data been gathered?
<--- Score

17. What successful thing are you doing today that may be blinding you to new growth opportunities?
<--- Score

18. Is the performance gap determined?
<--- Score

19. What is the common data model and what roles does it play with Dynamics 365?
<--- Score

20. Do several people in different organizational units assist with the Microsoft Dynamics 365 for Finance and Operations process?
<--- Score

21. What resources go in to get the desired output?
<--- Score

22. Is there an established change management process?
<--- Score

23. How are the new Business Process Flows exposed on the client side?
<--- Score

24. How many input/output points does it require?
<--- Score

25. What is the cost of poor quality as supported by the team's analysis?
<--- Score

26. What is the Common Data Service and what role does it play with Dynamics 365?
<--- Score

27. Should you invest in industry-recognized qualifications?
<--- Score

28. Is the suppliers process defined and controlled?
<--- Score

29. How will one upload new data to the service to refresh the existing data?
<--- Score

30. How long will the data reside in your solution?
<--- Score

31. Have you provided quick links and contact information?
<--- Score

32. How does database as a service make sense for an enterprise like your organization?
<--- Score

33. What are the customer needs that drive corresponding requirements?
<--- Score

34. Is there any way to speed up the process?
<--- Score

35. Why is customer engagement additional database storage changing?
<--- Score

36. How do you define collaboration and team output?
<--- Score

37. What were the crucial 'moments of truth' on the process map?
<--- Score

38. How is data used for program management and improvement?
<--- Score

39. Who will facilitate the team and process?
<--- Score

40. What are your Microsoft Dynamics 365 for Finance and Operations processes?
<--- Score

41. What tools were used to narrow the list of possible

causes?
<--- Score

42. Is the final output clearly identified?
<--- Score

43. How do you ensure that the Microsoft Dynamics 365 for Finance and Operations opportunity is realistic?
<--- Score

44. How do you leverage robotics, automation, and intelligence to get more value from your data?
<--- Score

45. How will corresponding data be collected?
<--- Score

46. Do you have the authority to produce the output?
<--- Score

47. Was a detailed process map created to amplify critical steps of the 'as is' stakeholder process?
<--- Score

48. How do your work systems and key work processes relate to and capitalize on your core competencies?
<--- Score

49. Can you add value to the current Microsoft Dynamics 365 for Finance and Operations decision-making process (largely qualitative) by incorporating uncertainty modeling (more quantitative)?
<--- Score

50. What is your organizations system for selecting qualified vendors?
<--- Score

51. What are the Microsoft Dynamics 365 for Finance and Operations design outputs?
<--- Score

52. Record-keeping requirements flow from the records needed as inputs, outputs, controls and for transformation of a Microsoft Dynamics 365 for Finance and Operations process, are the records needed as inputs to the Microsoft Dynamics 365 for Finance and Operations process available?
<--- Score

53. Are Microsoft Dynamics 365 for Finance and Operations changes recognized early enough to be approved through the regular process?
<--- Score

54. What other organizational variables, such as reward systems or communication systems, affect the performance of this Microsoft Dynamics 365 for Finance and Operations process?
<--- Score

55. What systems/processes must you excel at?
<--- Score

56. Why is unified operations database storage changing?
<--- Score

57. Have any additional benefits been identified that will result from closing all or most of the gaps?

<--- Score

58. How will the data be checked for quality?
<--- Score

59. How much data can be collected in the given timeframe?
<--- Score

60. How do you save time and money on the invoicing process?
<--- Score

61. Should you build a data warehouse?
<--- Score

62. Do you, as a leader, bounce back quickly from setbacks?
<--- Score

63. How is Microsoft Dynamics 365 for Finance and Operations data gathered?
<--- Score

64. What qualifications, experiences, achievements, and skills do you bring to a organization?
<--- Score

65. How is the Microsoft Dynamics 365 for Finance and Operations Value Stream Mapping managed?
<--- Score

66. Are all staff in core Microsoft Dynamics 365 for Finance and Operations subjects Highly Qualified?
<--- Score

67. What will drive Microsoft Dynamics 365 for Finance and Operations change?
<--- Score

68. What are your outputs?
<--- Score

69. What do you need to qualify?
<--- Score

70. How do you implement and manage your work processes to ensure that they meet design requirements?
<--- Score

71. What, related to, Microsoft Dynamics 365 for Finance and Operations processes does your organization outsource?
<--- Score

72. What level of latency are you comfortable with in accessing the data?
<--- Score

73. Who qualifies to gain access to data?
<--- Score

74. Do quality systems drive continuous improvement?
<--- Score

75. Do your employees have the opportunity to do what they do best everyday?
<--- Score

76. Do your leaders quickly bounce back from setbacks?
<--- Score

77. Where is the trigger for your process?
<--- Score

78. Did any additional data need to be collected?
<--- Score

79. What other jobs or tasks affect the performance of the steps in the Microsoft Dynamics 365 for Finance and Operations process?
<--- Score

80. What controls do you have in place to protect data?
<--- Score

81. Were there any improvement opportunities identified from the process analysis?
<--- Score

82. What training and qualifications will you need?
<--- Score

83. What is your organizations process which leads to recognition of value generation?
<--- Score

84. How much database storage is provided by default?
<--- Score

85. What conclusions were drawn from the team's data collection and analysis? How did the team reach

these conclusions?
<--- Score

86. What kinds of faults do you find in streams of data?
<--- Score

87. Which factors should be considered for delivery data control functionality?
<--- Score

88. What methods do you use to gather Microsoft Dynamics 365 for Finance and Operations data?
<--- Score

89. Is there any information about security, and who will have access and what access to the database while busy with the upgrade?
<--- Score

90. Where can you get qualified talent today?
<--- Score

91. How is the way you as the leader think and process information affecting your organizational culture?
<--- Score

92. How often will data be collected for measures?
<--- Score

93. What is the oversight process?
<--- Score

94. Are there any apps that can handle quick attendance taking or registration?
<--- Score

95. What are the Microsoft Dynamics 365 for Finance and Operations business drivers?
<--- Score

96. What did the team gain from developing a sub-process map?
<--- Score

97. Which Microsoft Dynamics 365 for Finance and Operations data should be retained?
<--- Score

98. What does the data say about the performance of the stakeholder process?
<--- Score

99. Do you put more than one source of data?
<--- Score

100. What output to create?
<--- Score

101. Where is Microsoft Dynamics 365 for Finance and Operations data gathered?
<--- Score

102. Were any designed experiments used to generate additional insight into the data analysis?
<--- Score

103. What are the changes in the functionality and process flows of the architecture?
<--- Score

104. How are outputs preserved and protected?

<--- Score

105. What Microsoft Dynamics 365 for Finance and Operations data will be collected?
<--- Score

106. Did any value-added analysis or 'lean thinking' take place to identify some of the gaps shown on the 'as is' process map?
<--- Score

107. How much data will you be ingesting?
<--- Score

108. Do you enable Editable Grids for only certain views of the data?
<--- Score

109. Is the gap/opportunity displayed and communicated in financial terms?
<--- Score

110. What kind of crime could a potential new hire have committed that would not only not disqualify him/her from being hired by your organization, but would actually indicate that he/she might be a particularly good fit?
<--- Score

111. What are evaluation criteria for the output?
<--- Score

112. When should a process be art not science?
<--- Score

113. How do the test cases treat input datasets and

expected outcomes?
<--- Score

114. What Microsoft Dynamics 365 for Finance and Operations data should be managed?
<--- Score

115. Is the Microsoft Dynamics 365 for Finance and Operations process severely broken such that a re-design is necessary?
<--- Score

116. What are the revised rough estimates of the financial savings/opportunity for Microsoft Dynamics 365 for Finance and Operations improvements?
<--- Score

117. Identify an operational issue in your organization, for example, could a particular task be done more quickly or more efficiently by Microsoft Dynamics 365 for Finance and Operations?
<--- Score

118. Is data and process analysis, root cause analysis and quantifying the gap/opportunity in place?
<--- Score

119. What qualifications do Microsoft Dynamics 365 for Finance and Operations leaders need?
<--- Score

120. How does common data service work?
<--- Score

121. How was the detailed process map generated, verified, and validated?

<--- Score

122. Is pre-qualification of suppliers carried out?
<--- Score

123. What qualifications and skills do you need?
<--- Score

124. Are all team members qualified for all tasks?
<--- Score

125. Have the problem and goal statements been updated to reflect the additional knowledge gained from the analyze phase?
<--- Score

126. What tools were used to generate the list of possible causes?
<--- Score

127. What process improvements will be needed?
<--- Score

128. Is special know how required to complete the test cases with your own data?
<--- Score

129. What were the financial benefits resulting from any 'ground fruit or low-hanging fruit' (quick fixes)?
<--- Score

130. Is there a limit on the database size that can be uploaded?
<--- Score

131. How does process mapping help with risk

management?
<--- Score

132. Is there any data encryption feature in the new release of mobile App for Dynamics 365?
<--- Score

Add up total points for this section:
_____ = Total points for this section

Divided by: ______ (number of statements answered) = ______ Average score for this section

Transfer your score to the Microsoft Dynamics 365 for Finance and Operations Index at the beginning of the Self-Assessment.

CRITERION #5: IMPROVE:

INTENT: Develop a practical solution. Innovate, establish and test the solution and to measure the results.

In my belief, the answer to this question is clearly defined:

5 Strongly Agree

4 Agree

3 Neutral

2 Disagree

1 Strongly Disagree

1. What is included in the new Microsoft Relationship Sales solution SKUs?
<--- Score

2. Are improved process ('should be') maps modified based on pilot data and analysis?
<--- Score

3. What strategies for Microsoft Dynamics 365 for

Finance and Operations improvement are successful?
<--- Score

4. How do you measure improved Microsoft Dynamics 365 for Finance and Operations service perception, and satisfaction?
<--- Score

5. Are the best solutions selected?
<--- Score

6. Was a pilot designed for the proposed solution(s)?
<--- Score

7. What is the team's contingency plan for potential problems occurring in implementation?
<--- Score

8. How are policy decisions made and where?
<--- Score

9. How will the group know that the solution worked?
<--- Score

10. Are records of inventory results with appropriate information maintained?
<--- Score

11. Is the Microsoft Dynamics 365 for Finance and Operations solution sustainable?
<--- Score

12. How do you mitigate Microsoft Dynamics 365 for Finance and Operations risk?
<--- Score

13. What tools were most useful during the improve phase?
<--- Score

14. How do you deal with Microsoft Dynamics 365 for Finance and Operations risk?
<--- Score

15. What can you do to improve?
<--- Score

16. Is the scope clearly documented?
<--- Score

17. Are the risks fully understood, reasonable and manageable?
<--- Score

18. What risks do you need to manage?
<--- Score

19. What actually has to improve and by how much?
<--- Score

20. Have you run into regulatory issues with having an aging software solution?
<--- Score

21. How do you go about comparing Microsoft Dynamics 365 for Finance and Operations approaches/solutions?
<--- Score

22. What are the implications of the one critical Microsoft Dynamics 365 for Finance and Operations decision 10 minutes, 10 months, and 10 years from

now?
<--- Score

23. What areas of your implementation pose a performance or reliability risk?
<--- Score

24. How can you better manage risk?
<--- Score

25. How do you improve productivity?
<--- Score

26. What are the Microsoft Dynamics 365 for Finance and Operations security risks?
<--- Score

27. How will you know that a change is an improvement?
<--- Score

28. Do you combine technical expertise with business knowledge and Microsoft Dynamics 365 for Finance and Operations Key topics include lifecycles, development approaches, requirements and how to make a business case?
<--- Score

29. What resources are required for the improvement efforts?
<--- Score

30. What attendant changes will need to be made to ensure that the solution is successful?
<--- Score

31. Are risk triggers captured?
<--- Score

32. What went well, what should change, what can improve?
<--- Score

33. What is enterprise risk management?
<--- Score

34. How will you know when its improved?
<--- Score

35. Who should make the Microsoft Dynamics 365 for Finance and Operations decisions?
<--- Score

36. What is the risk?
<--- Score

37. Who manages supplier risk management in your organization?
<--- Score

38. What to do with the results or outcomes of measurements?
<--- Score

39. What was the result of the more efficient record keeping system one developed?
<--- Score

40. Is the optimal solution selected based on testing and analysis?
<--- Score

41. How do you manage and improve your Microsoft Dynamics 365 for Finance and Operations work systems to deliver customer value and achieve organizational success and sustainability?
<--- Score

42. What lessons, if any, from a pilot were incorporated into the design of the full-scale solution?
<--- Score

43. How can skill-level changes improve Microsoft Dynamics 365 for Finance and Operations?
<--- Score

44. Are procedures documented for managing Microsoft Dynamics 365 for Finance and Operations risks?
<--- Score

45. What does the 'should be' process map/design look like?
<--- Score

46. Do you have the optimal project management team structure?
<--- Score

47. What current systems have to be understood and/or changed?
<--- Score

48. What is Microsoft Dynamics 365 for Finance and Operations's impact on utilizing the best solution(s)?
<--- Score

49. Is there a small-scale pilot for proposed

improvement(s)? What conclusions were drawn from the outcomes of a pilot?
<--- Score

50. How do you link measurement and risk?
<--- Score

51. Does apache harmony code have any role with respect to the development of the android platform?
<--- Score

52. Is pilot data collected and analyzed?
<--- Score

53. How do you measure progress and evaluate training effectiveness?
<--- Score

54. What is the implementation plan?
<--- Score

55. Which of the recognised risks out of all risks can be most likely transferred?
<--- Score

56. What were the underlying assumptions on the cost-benefit analysis?
<--- Score

57. How are Microsoft Dynamics 365 for Finance and Operations risks managed?
<--- Score

58. What error proofing will be done to address some of the discrepancies observed in the 'as is' process?

<--- Score

59. What area needs the greatest improvement?
<--- Score

60. Do you cover the five essential competencies: Communication, Collaboration,Innovation, Adaptability, and Leadership that improve an organizations ability to leverage the new Microsoft Dynamics 365 for Finance and Operations in a volatile global economy?
<--- Score

61. Have you achieved Microsoft Dynamics 365 for Finance and Operations improvements?
<--- Score

62. Is the implementation plan designed?
<--- Score

63. What were the criteria for evaluating a Microsoft Dynamics 365 for Finance and Operations pilot?
<--- Score

64. Who are the key stakeholders for the Microsoft Dynamics 365 for Finance and Operations evaluation?
<--- Score

65. What is the Microsoft Dynamics 365 for Finance and Operations's sustainability risk?
<--- Score

66. What practices helps your organization to develop its capacity to recognize patterns?
<--- Score

67. Who are the Microsoft Dynamics 365 for Finance and Operations decision makers?
<--- Score

68. Is there a high likelihood that any recommendations will achieve their intended results?
<--- Score

69. Who are the Microsoft Dynamics 365 for Finance and Operations decision-makers?
<--- Score

70. Who will be responsible for making the decisions to include or exclude requested changes once Microsoft Dynamics 365 for Finance and Operations is underway?
<--- Score

71. Is Microsoft Dynamics 365 for Finance and Operations documentation maintained?
<--- Score

72. What is Microsoft Dynamics 365 for Finance and Operations risk?
<--- Score

73. Is risk periodically assessed?
<--- Score

74. How is continuous improvement applied to risk management?
<--- Score

75. Does the software come with a tool to develop reports?
<--- Score

76. Is there a cost/benefit analysis of optimal solution(s)?
<--- Score

77. Explorations of the frontiers of Microsoft Dynamics 365 for Finance and Operations will help you build influence, improve Microsoft Dynamics 365 for Finance and Operations, optimize decision making, and sustain change, what is your approach?
<--- Score

78. What are the expected Microsoft Dynamics 365 for Finance and Operations results?
<--- Score

79. If you could go back in time five years, what decision would you make differently? What is your best guess as to what decision you're making today you might regret five years from now?
<--- Score

80. Who makes the Microsoft Dynamics 365 for Finance and Operations decisions in your organization?
<--- Score

81. How do you define the solutions' scope?
<--- Score

82. Can you identify any significant risks or exposures to Microsoft Dynamics 365 for Finance and Operations third- parties (vendors, service providers, alliance partners etc) that concern you?
<--- Score

83. What attracted you to mobile app development?
<--- Score

84. How scalable is your Microsoft Dynamics 365 for Finance and Operations solution?
<--- Score

85. What do you want to improve?
<--- Score

86. Is any Microsoft Dynamics 365 for Finance and Operations documentation required?
<--- Score

87. What should a proof of concept or pilot accomplish?
<--- Score

88. Is a solution implementation plan established, including schedule/work breakdown structure, resources, risk management plan, cost/budget, and control plan?
<--- Score

89. What assumptions are made about the solution and approach?
<--- Score

90. Are possible solutions generated and tested?
<--- Score

91. What alternative responses are available to manage risk?
<--- Score

92. Who do you report Microsoft Dynamics 365 for Finance and Operations results to?
<--- Score

93. Have you identified breakpoints and/or risk tolerances that will trigger broad consideration of a potential need for intervention or modification of strategy?
<--- Score

94. How else does an ERP system help with risk management?
<--- Score

95. How do you improve your likelihood of success ?
<--- Score

96. Were any criteria developed to assist the team in testing and evaluating potential solutions?
<--- Score

97. How do the Microsoft Dynamics 365 for Finance and Operations results compare with the performance of your competitors and other organizations with similar offerings?
<--- Score

98. How has your work experience influenced your decision?
<--- Score

99. How does your organization evaluate strategic Microsoft Dynamics 365 for Finance and Operations success?
<--- Score

100. How is knowledge sharing about risk management improved?
<--- Score

101. At what point will vulnerability assessments be performed once Microsoft Dynamics 365 for Finance and Operations is put into production (e.g., ongoing Risk Management after implementation)?
<--- Score

102. Are decisions made in a timely manner?
<--- Score

103. Can you integrate quality management and risk management?
<--- Score

104. Do you have an understanding of whether that number of developers has increased over time?
<--- Score

105. How did the team generate the list of possible solutions?
<--- Score

106. Are events managed to resolution?
<--- Score

107. Are new and improved process ('should be') maps developed?
<--- Score

108. Are the key business and technology risks being managed?
<--- Score

109. How do you manage Microsoft Dynamics 365 for Finance and Operations risk?
<--- Score

110. How will the team or the process owner(s) monitor the implementation plan to see that it is working as intended?
<--- Score

111. Is there any other Microsoft Dynamics 365 for Finance and Operations solution?
<--- Score

112. What tools were used to evaluate the potential solutions?
<--- Score

113. Describe the design of the pilot and what tests were conducted, if any?
<--- Score

114. How significant is the improvement in the eyes of the end user?
<--- Score

115. What criteria will you use to assess your Microsoft Dynamics 365 for Finance and Operations risks?
<--- Score

116. What communications are necessary to support the implementation of the solution?
<--- Score

117. Do those selected for the Microsoft Dynamics 365 for Finance and Operations team have a good

general understanding of what Microsoft Dynamics 365 for Finance and Operations is all about?
<--- Score

118. Are the most efficient solutions problem-specific?
<--- Score

119. Does the goal represent a desired result that can be measured?
<--- Score

120. How risky is your organization?
<--- Score

121. What improvements have been achieved?
<--- Score

122. How does the solution remove the key sources of issues discovered in the analyze phase?
<--- Score

123. Is a contingency plan established?
<--- Score

124. Can the solution be designed and implemented within an acceptable time period?
<--- Score

125. Are risk management tasks balanced centrally and locally?
<--- Score

126. What tools were used to tap into the creativity and encourage 'outside the box' thinking?
<--- Score

127. For decision problems, how do you develop a decision statement?
<--- Score

128. Who controls key decisions that will be made?
<--- Score

129. What needs improvement? Why?
<--- Score

130. Are there any constraints (technical, political, cultural, or otherwise) that would inhibit certain solutions?
<--- Score

Add up total points for this section:
_____ = Total points for this section

Divided by: ______ (number of statements answered) = ______ Average score for this section

Transfer your score to the Microsoft Dynamics 365 for Finance and Operations Index at the beginning of the Self-Assessment.

CRITERION #6: CONTROL:

INTENT: Implement the practical solution. Maintain the performance and correct possible complications.

In my belief, the answer to this question is clearly defined:

5 Strongly Agree

4 Agree

3 Neutral

2 Disagree

1 Strongly Disagree

1. How might the group capture best practices and lessons learned so as to leverage improvements?
<--- Score

2. Are operating procedures consistent?
<--- Score

3. How will the day-to-day responsibilities for monitoring and continual improvement be

transferred from the improvement team to the process owner?
<--- Score

4. Do the Microsoft Dynamics 365 for Finance and Operations decisions you make today help people and the planet tomorrow?
<--- Score

5. Can learning paths be driven by security role?
<--- Score

6. How do your controls stack up?
<--- Score

7. Are there any plans for the tracking to be available for emails created in Outlook?
<--- Score

8. Are pertinent alerts monitored, analyzed and distributed to appropriate personnel?
<--- Score

9. Can support from partners be adjusted?
<--- Score

10. What is the recommended frequency of auditing?
<--- Score

11. What other areas of the group might benefit from the Microsoft Dynamics 365 for Finance and Operations team's improvements, knowledge, and learning?
<--- Score

12. Is there a Microsoft Dynamics 365 for Finance and

Operations Communication plan covering who needs to get what information when?
<--- Score

13. What should the next improvement project be that is related to Microsoft Dynamics 365 for Finance and Operations?
<--- Score

14. Is there a recommended audit plan for routine surveillance inspections of Microsoft Dynamics 365 for Finance and Operations's gains?
<--- Score

15. Is the overall move to the cloud environment reflecting what was expected?
<--- Score

16. Will marketing be included in customer engagement plan?
<--- Score

17. What is your theory of human motivation, and how does your compensation plan fit with that view?
<--- Score

18. How will new or emerging customer needs/ requirements be checked/communicated to orient the process toward meeting the new specifications and continually reducing variation?
<--- Score

19. Is there documentation that will support the successful operation of the improvement?
<--- Score

20. Where do you plan on hosting your data, locally or in the cloud?
<--- Score

21. Are there device-based Plan(s) subscriptions?
<--- Score

22. Does the response plan contain a definite closed loop continual improvement scheme (e.g., plan-do-check-act)?
<--- Score

23. Will customers marketing activities be monitored?
<--- Score

24. What do you stand for--and what are you against?
<--- Score

25. What is the control/monitoring plan?
<--- Score

26. What are the known security controls?
<--- Score

27. Are the Microsoft Dynamics 365 for Finance and Operations standards challenging?
<--- Score

28. What are the companies doing to create a standardized semantic data model for digital marketing?
<--- Score

29. Act/Adjust: What Do you Need to Do Differently?
<--- Score

30. Does customer insights provide any form of machine learning?
<--- Score

31. What regulations and standards does your solution need to meet?
<--- Score

32. What key inputs and outputs are being measured on an ongoing basis?
<--- Score

33. Do you customize the system learning paths?
<--- Score

34. Does job training on the documented procedures need to be part of the process team's education and training?
<--- Score

35. Who will be in control?
<--- Score

36. Is there a standardized process?
<--- Score

37. Is there an action plan in case of emergencies?
<--- Score

38. Can you adapt and adjust to changing Microsoft Dynamics 365 for Finance and Operations situations?
<--- Score

39. Will any special training be provided for results interpretation?

<--- Score

40. How do senior leaders actions reflect a commitment to the organizations Microsoft Dynamics 365 for Finance and Operations values?
<--- Score

41. Will existing staff require re-training, for example, to learn new business processes?
<--- Score

42. Who controls critical resources?
<--- Score

43. Is there a transfer of ownership and knowledge to process owner and process team tasked with the responsibilities.
<--- Score

44. Are documented procedures clear and easy to follow for the operators?
<--- Score

45. Can a customer have a mix of plans?
<--- Score

46. Will the team be available to assist members in planning investigations?
<--- Score

47. How will input, process, and output variables be checked to detect for sub-optimal conditions?
<--- Score

48. Are you measuring, monitoring and predicting Microsoft Dynamics 365 for Finance and Operations

activities to optimize operations and profitability, and enhancing outcomes?
<--- Score

49. What did you learn from work experiences?
<--- Score

50. Is a response plan established and deployed?
<--- Score

51. What are the Power BI rights included with Dynamics 365 Customer Engagement Plan?
<--- Score

52. Has the improved process and its steps been standardized?
<--- Score

53. Do you configure learning paths for your custom entities?
<--- Score

54. Is a response plan in place for when the input, process, or output measures indicate an 'out-of-control' condition?
<--- Score

55. How will report readings be checked to effectively monitor performance?
<--- Score

56. Is there a control plan in place for sustaining improvements (short and long-term)?
<--- Score

57. Have new or revised work instructions resulted?

<--- Score

58. How do you select, collect, align, and integrate Microsoft Dynamics 365 for Finance and Operations data and information for tracking daily operations and overall organizational performance, including progress relative to strategic objectives and action plans?
<--- Score

59. What quality tools were useful in the control phase?
<--- Score

60. What can you control?
<--- Score

61. What do you measure to verify effectiveness gains?
<--- Score

62. What should you measure to verify efficiency gains?
<--- Score

63. Do the viable solutions scale to future needs?
<--- Score

64. Is there a documented and implemented monitoring plan?
<--- Score

65. How will you measure your QA plan's effectiveness?
<--- Score

66. What Microsoft Dynamics 365 for Finance and Operations standards are applicable?
<--- Score

67. Against what alternative is success being measured?
<--- Score

68. Are new process steps, standards, and documentation ingrained into normal operations?
<--- Score

69. How do controls support value?
<--- Score

70. How will the process owner verify improvement in present and future sigma levels, process capabilities?
<--- Score

71. Which budget planning feature should you use to identify the steps?
<--- Score

72. Do your grades accurately reflect your ability?
<--- Score

73. What other systems, operations, processes, and infrastructures (hiring practices, staffing, training, incentives/rewards, metrics/dashboards/scorecards, etc.) need updates, additions, changes, or deletions in order to facilitate knowledge transfer and improvements?
<--- Score

74. Has the Microsoft Dynamics 365 for Finance and Operations value of standards been quantified?

<--- Score

75. How can you best use all of your knowledge repositories to enhance learning and sharing?
<--- Score

76. Is there a documented investigative plan?
<--- Score

77. Who is the Microsoft Dynamics 365 for Finance and Operations process owner?
<--- Score

78. What are the critical parameters to watch?
<--- Score

79. Are suggested corrective/restorative actions indicated on the response plan for known causes to problems that might surface?
<--- Score

80. How often do you anticipate needing to scale your solution up or down?
<--- Score

81. Is knowledge gained on process shared and institutionalized?
<--- Score

82. What should you include in the plan?
<--- Score

83. Are there documented procedures?
<--- Score

84. How will Microsoft Dynamics 365 for Finance and

Operations decisions be made and monitored?
<--- Score

85. How will the process owner and team be able to hold the gains?
<--- Score

86. What are your results for key measures or indicators of the accomplishment of your Microsoft Dynamics 365 for Finance and Operations strategy and action plans, including building and strengthening core competencies?
<--- Score

87. You may have created your quality measures at a time when you lacked resources, technology wasn't up to the required standard, or low service levels were the industry norm. Have those circumstances changed?
<--- Score

88. Does the Microsoft Dynamics 365 for Finance and Operations performance meet the customer's requirements?
<--- Score

89. Is reporting being used or needed?
<--- Score

90. How do you control security roles across the different apps?
<--- Score

91. What is the standard for acceptable Microsoft Dynamics 365 for Finance and Operations performance?

<--- Score

92. What are you attempting to measure/monitor?
<--- Score

93. Does a troubleshooting guide exist or is it needed?
<--- Score

94. Does your organization have plans for expansion?
<--- Score

95. What is your plan to assess your security risks?
<--- Score

96. Where do you find detailed information about functionality licensed via Applications, Plans, and Team Members subscriptions?
<--- Score

97. What is the purpose of the budget control feature in Microsoft Dynamics 365 for Finance and Operations?
<--- Score

98. Is new knowledge gained imbedded in the response plan?
<--- Score

Add up total points for this section:
_____ = Total points for this section

Divided by: ______ (number of statements answered) = ______ Average score for this section

Transfer your score to the Microsoft Dynamics 365 for Finance and Operations Index at the beginning of the Self-Assessment.

CRITERION #7: SUSTAIN:

INTENT: Retain the benefits.

In my belief, the answer to this question is clearly defined:

5 Strongly Agree

4 Agree

3 Neutral

2 Disagree

1 Strongly Disagree

1. How do you get ready for Dynamics 365?
<--- Score

2. What is the location of servers?
<--- Score

3. What are cumulative service updates?
<--- Score

4. What counts that you are not counting?
<--- Score

5. What are the functions organizations?
<--- Score

6. Why not do Microsoft Dynamics 365 for Finance and Operations?
<--- Score

7. Will there be any necessary staff changes (redundancies or new hires)?
<--- Score

8. What are the potential basics of Microsoft Dynamics 365 for Finance and Operations fraud?
<--- Score

9. How much longer will your product be supported by Microsoft?
<--- Score

10. How do you listen to customers to obtain actionable information?
<--- Score

11. What unique value proposition (UVP) do you offer?
<--- Score

12. Do you add custom entities to scheduler?
<--- Score

13. What is Microsoft dynamics 365 business central?
<--- Score

14. Are you maintaining a past–present–future perspective throughout the Microsoft Dynamics 365

for Finance and Operations discussion?
<--- Score

15. What is your formula for success in Microsoft Dynamics 365 for Finance and Operations ?
<--- Score

16. Are Microsoft products under software assurance?
<--- Score

17. How does engineering training respond to realities?
<--- Score

18. What are specific Microsoft Dynamics 365 for Finance and Operations rules to follow?
<--- Score

19. How is the logic handled if the values are removed?
<--- Score

20. Do all corresponding Dynamics 365 apps really work together seamlessly?
<--- Score

21. Is market fragmentation harming market quality?
<--- Score

22. What is the best approach to moving forward?
<--- Score

23. What are the barriers to increased Microsoft Dynamics 365 for Finance and Operations

production?
<--- Score

24. How will you motivate the stakeholders with the least vested interest?
<--- Score

25. Why should you consider Dynamics 365 Business Central?
<--- Score

26. How does dynamics 365 benefit customers?
<--- Score

27. How do you proactively clarify deliverables and Microsoft Dynamics 365 for Finance and Operations quality expectations?
<--- Score

28. What are current Microsoft Dynamics 365 for Finance and Operations paradigms?
<--- Score

29. Is project service integrated with operations in dynamics 365?
<--- Score

30. What options do you offer customers that do not want to go the cloud?
<--- Score

31. How does your organization be helpful in making typical day go more smoothly?
<--- Score

32. What are the options of on premises customers

renewing to the Dynamics 365 in the cloud?
<--- Score

33. Are orders currently being run through Microsoft Dynamics 365?
<--- Score

34. What are strategies for increasing support and reducing opposition?
<--- Score

35. Operational - will it work?
<--- Score

36. What is your Microsoft Dynamics 365 for Finance and Operations strategy?
<--- Score

37. Who are the key stakeholders?
<--- Score

38. Are you likely to stay on the job for a reasonable period of time and be productive?
<--- Score

39. Will it be accepted by users?
<--- Score

40. Can web resources also be used in the mobile app?
<--- Score

41. Is the editable grid available for custom entities?
<--- Score

42. How may dynamics 365 smb offer customers transition to dynamics 365 online skus?
<--- Score

43. Do you have to go to a branch to open an account?
<--- Score

44. Are skills and education taken into account?
<--- Score

45. What are the long-term Microsoft Dynamics 365 for Finance and Operations goals?
<--- Score

46. What are the business goals Microsoft Dynamics 365 for Finance and Operations is aiming to achieve?
<--- Score

47. How can you incorporate support to ensure safe and effective use of Microsoft Dynamics 365 for Finance and Operations into the services that you provide?
<--- Score

48. How many personnel will it take to perform duties?
<--- Score

49. What do you do in your roles as an executive in your organization?
<--- Score

50. What is your organizations main industry?
<--- Score

51. Who are four people whose careers you have enhanced?
<--- Score

52. When may a customer reduce the number of marketable contacts?
<--- Score

53. Which Microsoft Dynamics 365 for Finance and Operations goals are the most important?
<--- Score

54. What is the recommended frequency of auditing?
<--- Score

55. Are the criteria for selecting recommendations stated?
<--- Score

56. How does advanced warehouse management help?
<--- Score

57. How are you doing compared to your industry?
<--- Score

58. What is the path to Dynamics 365 for existing online and on premises customers?
<--- Score

59. What do leading companies look for in new enterprise systems?
<--- Score

60. Do you prefer large or small organizations?
<--- Score

61. What is appropriate for the specific situation?
<--- Score

62. What factors should you take into account in deciding on an investment strategy?
<--- Score

63. Do you see the system in action?
<--- Score

64. How do you keep records, of what?
<--- Score

65. Are users dispersed over multiple geographically located sites?
<--- Score

66. What purpose do you assign to your organizational hierarchy?
<--- Score

67. Are sales professional users able to increase customizations limits?
<--- Score

68. What is Microsoft dynamics 365 for finance and operations, enterprise edition?
<--- Score

69. Why is Microsoft Dynamics 365 for Finance and Operations important for you now?
<--- Score

70. How can you become the company that would put you out of business?

<--- Score

71. What is a feasible sequencing of reform initiatives over time?
<--- Score

72. What are internal and external Microsoft Dynamics 365 for Finance and Operations relations?
<--- Score

73. Do your employees work in functions that would benefit from collaboration with colleagues?
<--- Score

74. Do you keep your on-premises Dynamics 365 installation?
<--- Score

75. What education or training supports your job objective?
<--- Score

76. If your customer were your grandmother, would you tell her to buy what you're selling?
<--- Score

77. What is the biggest challenge facing your organization?
<--- Score

78. How many purchase orders does your organization generate each month?
<--- Score

79. Who is on the team?
<--- Score

80. Do you briefly summarize the different modules that are available in the system?
<--- Score

81. How widespread is its use?
<--- Score

82. What type of file storage is included?
<--- Score

83. What is the purpose of Microsoft Dynamics 365 for Finance and Operations in relation to the mission?
<--- Score

84. Is your organization environmentally conscious?
<--- Score

85. What does your business look like right now?
<--- Score

86. Is Microsoft Dynamics 365 for Finance and Operations realistic, or are you setting yourself up for failure?
<--- Score

87. Do you know what your customers value?
<--- Score

88. If you got fired and a new hire took your place, what would she do different?
<--- Score

89. How do you feel about working overtime?
<--- Score

90. How do you maintain Microsoft Dynamics 365 for Finance and Operations's Integrity?
<--- Score

91. How do you, as your organization, make the choice?
<--- Score

92. Is your business equipped to compete?
<--- Score

93. What was the last experiment you ran?
<--- Score

94. How are functional architectures of software products modelled?
<--- Score

95. What is the minimum time in which temporary systems may be expected to become available?
<--- Score

96. Do you know of any openings for a person with your skills?
<--- Score

97. How is email security and privacy are handled when it comes to relationship insights?
<--- Score

98. What you are going to do to affect the numbers?
<--- Score

99. What part does audit quality play?
<--- Score

100. Is your organization versatile in offering diverse services for the shipping industry?
<--- Score

101. Do you use Dynamics AX today mostly out of the box?
<--- Score

102. How do you serve your customers more effectively in the field?
<--- Score

103. How do you create buy-in?
<--- Score

104. What is the sentiment on products compared to competitors in the web and on social media?
<--- Score

105. Does your organization encourage further education?
<--- Score

106. How many licenses may a customer purchase at the better together prices?
<--- Score

107. Who do you think the world wants your organization to be?
<--- Score

108. What are your industrys challenges?
<--- Score

109. What is the funding source for this project?

<--- Score

110. What platform is Dynamics 365 running on?
<--- Score

111. Do you use present tense for current positions and past tense for past experiences?
<--- Score

112. Have you included all relevant work experience?
<--- Score

113. How will projects point the way to price convergence?
<--- Score

114. What will be the consequences to the stakeholder (financial, reputation etc) if Microsoft Dynamics 365 for Finance and Operations does not go ahead or fails to deliver the objectives?
<--- Score

115. How do you locate departments of interest?
<--- Score

116. How do you procure services for the cloud?
<--- Score

117. How do you know which account to choose?
<--- Score

118. Who, on the executive team or the board, has spoken to a customer recently?
<--- Score

119. Political -is anyone trying to undermine this project?
<--- Score

120. How does dynamics 365 finance and operations eliminate organization silos?
<--- Score

121. What are the rules and assumptions your industry operates under? What if the opposite were true?
<--- Score

122. Are session times presented in the time zone of the venue?
<--- Score

123. Are you willing to place custom code in Dynamics 365?
<--- Score

124. Why do and why don't your customers like your organization?
<--- Score

125. How will you insure seamless interoperability of Microsoft Dynamics 365 for Finance and Operations moving forward?
<--- Score

126. Ask yourself: how would you do this work if you only had one staff member to do it?
<--- Score

127. What is the purpose of a quality order in Microsoft Dynamics 365 for Finance and Operations?

<--- Score

128. What are the success criteria that will indicate that Microsoft Dynamics 365 for Finance and Operations objectives have been met and the benefits delivered?
<--- Score

129. What happens to your price for the team members already licensed?
<--- Score

130. What is the range of capabilities?
<--- Score

131. How will you know that the Microsoft Dynamics 365 for Finance and Operations project has been successful?
<--- Score

132. Is it economical; do you have the time and money?
<--- Score

133. Who will determine interim and final deadlines?
<--- Score

134. What happens to your existing reports and BI content when you move to Dynamics 365?
<--- Score

135. Is a single job application flow for executives and hourly employees desirable?
<--- Score

136. What is Microsoft dynamics 365 for finance

and operations?
<--- Score

137. Are you / should you be revolutionary or evolutionary?
<--- Score

138. What restrictions apply to particular accounts?
<--- Score

139. What do you get up to outside of work?
<--- Score

140. Who is responsible for Microsoft Dynamics 365 for Finance and Operations?
<--- Score

141. How did you handle personality conflicts with members of your organization?
<--- Score

142. Is there a work around that you can use?
<--- Score

143. What is your business doing right now?
<--- Score

144. What is the acceptable loss in functionality/ availability of your system?
<--- Score

145. What stupid rule would you most like to kill?
<--- Score

146. How long can current customers continue to

use Microsoft Dynamics Marketing?
<--- Score

147. Has there been any consideration of a delivery service?
<--- Score

148. What is the Core Function of the Project?
<--- Score

149. What kind of service account should you choose?
<--- Score

150. What is Microsoft Dynamics 365 for operations?
<--- Score

151. How do server side errors e.g. plug-in or workflows show with editable grids?
<--- Score

152. Is your strategy driving your strategy? Or is the way in which you allocate resources driving your strategy?
<--- Score

153. Is remote working right for your organization?
<--- Score

154. What are the key enablers to make this Microsoft Dynamics 365 for Finance and Operations move?
<--- Score

155. What have been your experiences in defining

long range Microsoft Dynamics 365 for Finance and Operations goals?
<--- Score

156. What security tools are provided in software?
<--- Score

157. How is implementation research currently incorporated into each of your goals?
<--- Score

158. How can you become more high-tech but still be high touch?
<--- Score

159. Have you ever encountered delays in your workflow due to an approver being out of office?
<--- Score

160. What changes are occurring for Dynamics in CSP?
<--- Score

161. How is your current system performing?
<--- Score

162. What do you do to modernize your business systems efficiently?
<--- Score

163. What is new with Microsoft Dynamics 365 for Operations?
<--- Score

164. Do you set regarding to customer entities?
<--- Score

165. How much contingency will be available in the budget?
<--- Score

166. What is dynamics 365 and how do you get it?
<--- Score

167. What are your personal philosophies regarding Microsoft Dynamics 365 for Finance and Operations and how do they influence your work?
<--- Score

168. Does your organization value creativity and individuality?
<--- Score

169. What is the craziest thing you can do?
<--- Score

170. Who else should you help?
<--- Score

171. Do you feel that more should be done in the Microsoft Dynamics 365 for Finance and Operations area?
<--- Score

172. Which is best for your business?
<--- Score

173. Whom among your colleagues do you trust, and for what?
<--- Score

174. Who have you, as a company, historically been

when you've been at your best?
<--- Score

175. What is effective Microsoft Dynamics 365 for Finance and Operations?
<--- Score

176. Do budgeting services continue all year long or just at certain times of the year?
<--- Score

177. Has all pertinent information been requested and received?
<--- Score

178. What is enterprise content management?
<--- Score

179. What is the quality level of professional skills in the account management team?
<--- Score

180. How is Microsofts erp system different?
<--- Score

181. Who is the main stakeholder, with ultimate responsibility for driving Microsoft Dynamics 365 for Finance and Operations forward?
<--- Score

182. Instead of going to current contacts for new ideas, what if you reconnected with dormant contacts--the people you used to know? If you were going reactivate a dormant tie, who would it be?
<--- Score

183. What business benefits will Microsoft Dynamics 365 for Finance and Operations goals deliver if achieved?
<--- Score

184. Do you have a robust cybersecurity program in place?
<--- Score

185. What is your favorite thing about working in your role?
<--- Score

186. Which models, tools and techniques are necessary?
<--- Score

187. How do you obtain training for your sales and technical teams?
<--- Score

188. Do you afford to wait for a managers approval?
<--- Score

189. Is nav the same thing as business central?
<--- Score

190. What tools do you use once you have decided on a Microsoft Dynamics 365 for Finance and Operations strategy and more importantly how do you choose?
<--- Score

191. Did the operator demonstrate safe handling and security during transportation, use and storage?

<--- Score

192. How does dynamics 365 finance and operations benefit customers?
<--- Score

193. Do you have past Microsoft Dynamics 365 for Finance and Operations successes?
<--- Score

194. How can Microsoft dynamics marketing customers transition to the new marketing app?
<--- Score

195. How do you accomplish your long range Microsoft Dynamics 365 for Finance and Operations goals?
<--- Score

196. Do you have experience with any types of companies?
<--- Score

197. How does the signals feature work with a queue mailbox?
<--- Score

198. How is Dynamics 365 for marketing licensed?
<--- Score

199. If you were responsible for initiating and implementing major changes in your organization, what steps might you take to ensure acceptance of those changes?
<--- Score

200. What is your BATNA (best alternative to a negotiated agreement)?
<--- Score

201. How do you make it meaningful in connecting Microsoft Dynamics 365 for Finance and Operations with what users do day-to-day?
<--- Score

202. Will Dynamics 365 be deployed as SaaS or iaas?
<--- Score

203. Does culture align with your organization culture?
<--- Score

204. How are service requests captured?
<--- Score

205. What is your enterprises current inventory of hardware and software?
<--- Score

206. What are your current barriers to adoption?
<--- Score

207. What experiences would make an entry level job seeker competitive?
<--- Score

208. What trophy do you want on your mantle?
<--- Score

209. How do you transition from the baseline to the target?

<--- Score

210. What other support options are available to customers directly from Microsoft?
<--- Score

211. Which way is the best for your business?
<--- Score

212. What is the next wave going to look like for Microsoft?
<--- Score

213. Are any of your organization employees unionized?
<--- Score

214. What skills and strengths do you have to offer your organization?
<--- Score

215. Are you too successful for your current ERP system?
<--- Score

216. Will customers email flow be stopped if the maximum is exceeded?
<--- Score

217. Did that come up from time to time?
<--- Score

218. Is the mobile App still using the HTML file storage?
<--- Score

219. How do you foster the skills, knowledge, talents, attributes, and characteristics you want to have?
<--- Score

220. Who is responsible for errors?
<--- Score

221. What happens when a new employee joins the organization?
<--- Score

222. What licensing channel is Dynamics 365 Business Central available?
<--- Score

223. Are you more comfortable as a team leader or team member?
<--- Score

224. What makes dynamics 365 exceptional?
<--- Score

225. How do you ensure that your organization has the right culture?
<--- Score

226. What application features should you use?
<--- Score

227. What is distributed order management?
<--- Score

228. How do you provide a safe environment -physically and emotionally?
<--- Score

229. Are the users satisfied with the performance and benefits of the IT Investment?
<--- Score

230. What is Microsofts industry strategy?
<--- Score

231. What are the essentials of internal Microsoft Dynamics 365 for Finance and Operations management?
<--- Score

232. Is there any intention to support multiple organizations per mailbox?
<--- Score

233. When is a device subscription more appropriate than a user subscription?
<--- Score

234. How much employee training have you been able to implement in order to increase product knowledge?
<--- Score

235. Is there a license with that software?
<--- Score

236. Why should people listen to you?
<--- Score

237. How do you lead with Microsoft Dynamics 365 for Finance and Operations in mind?
<--- Score

238. What kind of image is your organization

trying to present through branding?
<--- Score

239. Why will customers want to buy your organizations products/services?
<--- Score

240. How are new releases being communicated to the implementation partners?
<--- Score

241. What are the options of on premises customers renewing to the Dynamics 365 online?
<--- Score

242. What are the main characteristics of your organizations pursuing a quality management?
<--- Score

243. Is the free software movement a subset of the open source movement?
<--- Score

244. Do you share pricing information with potential customers?
<--- Score

245. Can debt be more expensive than it initially appears?
<--- Score

246. How Microsoft azure is a breakthrough in manufacturing?
<--- Score

247. Are you making progress, and are you making

progress as Microsoft Dynamics 365 for Finance and Operations leaders?
<--- Score

248. How do you ensure a great experience for your clients?
<--- Score

249. Is Microsoft social engagement part of dynamics 365?
<--- Score

250. What projects are going on in the organization today, and what resources are those projects using from the resource pools?
<--- Score

251. What is your vision for your organizations future?
<--- Score

252. How many users will be registered?
<--- Score

253. When and where will Dynamics 365 be available?
<--- Score

254. What is the maximum acceptable delay before which temporary systems must be made available?
<--- Score

255. How will team members knowledge management use rights change?
<--- Score

256. What one word do you want to own in the minds of your customers, employees, and partners?
<--- Score

257. Does the software provider or the user group manage the agenda and contents of the meetings?
<--- Score

258. Can field service be used for manufacturers who are doing own machine maintenance?
<--- Score

259. How do you use smart encryption techniques for cloud apps?
<--- Score

260. Do you prefer to work under supervision or on your own?
<--- Score

261. What happens if you do not have enough funding?
<--- Score

262. Do you step up from Dynamics 365 for Team Members to Dynamics 365 for Operations Activity?
<--- Score

263. How well does the model represent the given system or situation using semantics and syntax?
<--- Score

264. What is Dynamics 365 for team members subscription?
<--- Score

265. What information is critical to your organization that your executives are ignoring?
<--- Score

266. What is the kind of project structure that would be appropriate for your Microsoft Dynamics 365 for Finance and Operations project, should it be formal and complex, or can it be less formal and relatively simple?
<--- Score

267. Which product is right for your organization?
<--- Score

268. What is top of mind for supply chain operators?
<--- Score

269. Can corresponding apps be deployed to the mobile?
<--- Score

270. Is flow integrated with operations in Dynamics 365?
<--- Score

271. What could happen if you do not do it?
<--- Score

272. Why is it important to have senior management support for a Microsoft Dynamics 365 for Finance and Operations project?
<--- Score

273. How many work orders have been completed

by each field service engineer?
<--- Score

274. Are workflow custom activities available from Business Rules now?
<--- Score

275. How is the business doing overall?
<--- Score

276. What is the intended experience for your end user?
<--- Score

277. How do you set Microsoft Dynamics 365 for Finance and Operations stretch targets and how do you get people to not only participate in setting these stretch targets but also that they strive to achieve these?
<--- Score

278. Are editable grids available for custom entities?
<--- Score

279. Did the income earned from any particular occupation surprise you?
<--- Score

280. What is the type of evidence of the audit of the future?
<--- Score

281. What are the top 3 things at the forefront of your Microsoft Dynamics 365 for Finance and Operations agendas for the next 3 years?

<--- Score

282. Is there any reason to believe the opposite of my current belief?
<--- Score

283. What trouble can you get into?
<--- Score

284. How will you ensure you get what you expected?
<--- Score

285. Are the java apis part of the java programming language?
<--- Score

286. Are there different Dynamics 365 on Azure versions?
<--- Score

287. How competitive is the job market?
<--- Score

288. What is your favorite thing about marketing in the Microsoft Dynamics channel?
<--- Score

Add up total points for this section:
_____ = Total points for this section

Divided by: ______ (number of statements answered) = ______
Average score for this section

Transfer your score to the Microsoft Dynamics 365 for Finance and

Operations Index at the beginning of the Self-Assessment.

Microsoft Dynamics 365 For Finance And Operations and Managing Projects, Criteria for Project Managers:

1.0 Initiating Process Group: Microsoft Dynamics 365 For Finance And Operations

1. Who is funding the Microsoft Dynamics 365 For Finance And Operations project?

2. How can you make your needs known?

3. What must be done?

4. What are the pressing issues of the hour?

5. What areas were overlooked on this Microsoft Dynamics 365 For Finance And Operations project?

6. How do you help others satisfy needs?

7. The Microsoft Dynamics 365 For Finance And Operations project you are managing has nine stakeholders. How many channel of communications are there between corresponding stakeholders?

8. Who are the Microsoft Dynamics 365 For Finance And Operations project stakeholders?

9. When are the deliverables to be generated in each phase?

10. How will you know you did it?

11. How is each deliverable reviewed, verified, and validated?

12. Are identified risks being monitored properly, are new risks arising during the Microsoft Dynamics 365 For Finance And Operations project or are foreseen risks occurring?

13. What communication items need improvement?

14. Just how important is your work to the overall success of the Microsoft Dynamics 365 For Finance And Operations project?

15. Do you understand all business (operational), technical, resource and vendor risks associated with the Microsoft Dynamics 365 For Finance And Operations project?

16. First of all, should any action be taken?

17. Were escalated issues resolved promptly?

18. Were resources available as planned?

19. Have you evaluated the teams performance and asked for feedback?

20. How will it affect me?

1.1 Project Charter: Microsoft Dynamics 365 For Finance And Operations

21. Why the improvements?

22. What barriers do you predict to your success?

23. Dependent Microsoft Dynamics 365 For Finance And Operations projects: what Microsoft Dynamics 365 For Finance And Operations projects must be underway or completed before this Microsoft Dynamics 365 For Finance And Operations project can be successful?

24. How will you know a change is an improvement?

25. Why do you need to manage scope?

26. Why is a Microsoft Dynamics 365 For Finance And Operations project Charter used?

27. Avoid costs, improve service, and/ or comply with a mandate?

28. What is the business need?

29. Major high-level milestone targets: what events measure progress?

30. What are some examples of a business case?

31. What are the known stakeholder requirements?

32. Why have you chosen the aim you have set forth?

33. How will you learn more about the process or system you are trying to improve?

34. Run it as as a startup?

35. Did your Microsoft Dynamics 365 For Finance And Operations project ask for this?

36. When is a charter needed?

37. What are the assumptions?

38. How high should you set your goals?

39. Are there special technology requirements?

40. Why do you manage integration?

1.2 Stakeholder Register: Microsoft Dynamics 365 For Finance And Operations

41. Who is managing stakeholder engagement?

42. How big is the gap?

43. How should employers make voices heard?

44. What opportunities exist to provide communications?

45. What & Why?

46. Who are the stakeholders?

47. Is your organization ready for change?

48. What are the major Microsoft Dynamics 365 For Finance And Operations project milestones requiring communications or providing communications opportunities?

49. What is the power of the stakeholder?

50. How will reports be created?

51. Who wants to talk about Security?

52. How much influence do they have on the Microsoft Dynamics 365 For Finance And Operations project?

1.3 Stakeholder Analysis Matrix: Microsoft Dynamics 365 For Finance And Operations

53. Who is directly responsible for decisions on issues important to the Microsoft Dynamics 365 For Finance And Operations project?

54. How are the threatened Microsoft Dynamics 365 For Finance And Operations project targets being used?

55. Experience, knowledge, data?

56. Philosophy and values?

57. Who will be affected by the work?

58. Price, value, quality?

59. Who has not been involved up to now and should have been?

60. Contributions to policy and practice?

61. Who will obstruct/hinder the Microsoft Dynamics 365 For Finance And Operations project if they are not involved?

62. What is the relationship among stakeholders?

63. How are you predicting what future (work)loads will be?

64. Lack of competitive strength?

65. Which conditions out of the control of the management are crucial for the achievement of the outputs?

66. Vulnerable groups; who are the vulnerable groups that might be affected by the Microsoft Dynamics 365 For Finance And Operations project?

67. What obstacles does your organization face?

68. Innovative aspects?

69. Does the stakeholder want to be involved or merely need to be informed about the Microsoft Dynamics 365 For Finance And Operations project and its process?

70. What are the reimbursement requirements?

71. Continuity, supply chain robustness?

2.0 Planning Process Group: Microsoft Dynamics 365 For Finance And Operations

72. If a task is partitionable, is this a sufficient condition to reduce the Microsoft Dynamics 365 For Finance And Operations project duration?

73. How well will the chosen processes produce the expected results?

74. What do they need to know about the Microsoft Dynamics 365 For Finance And Operations project?

75. Microsoft Dynamics 365 For Finance And Operations project assessment; why did you do this Microsoft Dynamics 365 For Finance And Operations project?

76. In which Microsoft Dynamics 365 For Finance And Operations project management process group is the detailed Microsoft Dynamics 365 For Finance And Operations project budget created?

77. Contingency planning. if a risk event occurs, what will you do?

78. To what extent has the intervention strategy been adapted to the areas of intervention in which it is being implemented?

79. Is the Microsoft Dynamics 365 For Finance And Operations project supported by national and/or local

organizations?

80. Just how important is your work to the overall success of the Microsoft Dynamics 365 For Finance And Operations project?

81. To what extent and in what ways are the Microsoft Dynamics 365 For Finance And Operations project contributing to progress towards organizational reform?

82. How will it affect you?

83. Is the schedule for the set products being met?

84. Why is it important to determine activity sequencing on Microsoft Dynamics 365 For Finance And Operations projects?

85. What type of estimation method are you using?

86. How are it Microsoft Dynamics 365 For Finance And Operations projects different?

87. To what extent have the target population and participants made the activities own, taking an active role in it?

88. Is your organization showing technical capacity and leadership commitment to keep working with the Microsoft Dynamics 365 For Finance And Operations project and to repeat it?

89. What do you need to do?

90. What are the different approaches to building the

WBS?

91. Mitigate. what will you do to minimize the impact should a risk event occur?

2.1 Project Management Plan: Microsoft Dynamics 365 For Finance And Operations

92. Does the implementation plan have an appropriate division of responsibilities?

93. What does management expect of PMs?

94. What is risk management?

95. Who manages integration?

96. Why Change?

97. Is mitigation authorized or recommended?

98. Is there anything you would now do differently on your Microsoft Dynamics 365 For Finance And Operations project based on past experience?

99. What goes into your Microsoft Dynamics 365 For Finance And Operations project Charter?

100. What did not work so well?

101. Has the selected plan been formulated using cost effectiveness and incremental analysis techniques?

102. When is the Microsoft Dynamics 365 For Finance And Operations project management plan created?

103. Do there need to be organizational changes?

104. Does the selected plan protect privacy?

105. Are there non-structural buyout or relocation recommendations?

106. What data/reports/tools/etc. do program managers need?

107. Are there any windfall benefits that would accrue to the Microsoft Dynamics 365 For Finance And Operations project sponsor or other parties?

108. How do you organize the costs in the Microsoft Dynamics 365 For Finance And Operations project management plan?

109. If the Microsoft Dynamics 365 For Finance And Operations project is complex or scope is specialized, do you have appropriate and/or qualified staff available to perform the tasks?

110. How do you manage integration?

111. How can you best help your organization to develop consistent practices in Microsoft Dynamics 365 For Finance And Operations project management planning stages?

2.2 Scope Management Plan: Microsoft Dynamics 365 For Finance And Operations

112. Is there an issues management plan in place?

113. Personnel with expertise?

114. Describe the process for accepting the Microsoft Dynamics 365 For Finance And Operations project deliverables. Will the Microsoft Dynamics 365 For Finance And Operations project deliverables become accepted in writing?

115. Are risk triggers captured?

116. Is there a requirements change management processes in place?

117. Does the resource management plan include a personnel development plan?

118. What strengths do you have?

119. Will the Microsoft Dynamics 365 For Finance And Operations project deliverables become accepted in writing?

120. Have activity relationships and interdependencies within tasks been adequately identified?

121. Organizational policies that might affect the

availability of resources?

122. Are corrective actions taken when actual results are substantially different from detailed Microsoft Dynamics 365 For Finance And Operations project plan (variances)?

123. Have all documents been archived in a Microsoft Dynamics 365 For Finance And Operations project repository for each release?

124. Timeline and milestones?

125. Are calculations and results of analyzes essentially correct?

126. Have key stakeholders been identified?

127. What are the risks of not having good inter-organization cooperation on the Microsoft Dynamics 365 For Finance And Operations project?

128. How many changes are you making?

129. Has the business need been clearly defined?

130. Are staffing resource estimates sufficiently detailed and documented for use in planning and tracking the Microsoft Dynamics 365 For Finance And Operations project?

131. Has appropriate allowance been made for the effect of the learning curve on all personnel joining the Microsoft Dynamics 365 For Finance And Operations project who do not have the required prior industry, functional & technical expertise?

2.3 Requirements Management Plan: Microsoft Dynamics 365 For Finance And Operations

132. What cost metrics will be used?

133. Did you distinguish the scope of work the contractor(s) will be required to do?

134. Is the user satisfied?

135. Do you have price sheets and a methodology for determining the total proposal cost?

136. What performance metrics will be used?

137. Will the contractors involved take full responsibility?

138. Did you provide clear and concise specifications?

139. To see if a requirement statement is sufficiently well-defined, read it from the developers perspective. Mentally add the phrase, call me when youre done to the end of the requirement and see if that makes you nervous. In other words, would you need additional clarification from the author to understand the requirement well enough to design and implement it?

140. Will you document changes to requirements?

141. How often will the reporting occur?

142. Are all the stakeholders ready for the transition into the user community?

143. Who will initially review the Microsoft Dynamics 365 For Finance And Operations project work or products to ensure it meets the applicable acceptance criteria?

144. Could inaccurate or incomplete requirements in this Microsoft Dynamics 365 For Finance And Operations project create a serious risk for the business?

145. Have stakeholders been instructed in the Change Control process?

146. Is requirements work dependent on any other specific Microsoft Dynamics 365 For Finance And Operations project or non-Microsoft Dynamics 365 For Finance And Operations project activities (e.g. funding, approvals, procurement)?

147. What are you trying to do?

148. Is the system software (non-operating system) new to the IT Microsoft Dynamics 365 For Finance And Operations project team?

149. Should you include sub-activities?

150. How will unresolved questions be handled once approval has been obtained?

151. Who will finally present the work or product(s) for acceptance?

2.4 Requirements Documentation: Microsoft Dynamics 365 For Finance And Operations

152. Who is interacting with the system?

153. Completeness. are all functions required by the customer included?

154. Are there any requirements conflicts?

155. Where do system and software requirements come from, what are sources?

156. Who provides requirements?

157. What kind of entity is a problem ?

158. How does what is being described meet the business need?

159. Is the requirement properly understood?

160. Does your organization restrict technical alternatives?

161. Verifiability. can the requirements be checked?

162. Do your constraints stand?

163. Where do you define what is a customer, what are the attributes of customer?

164. Has requirements gathering uncovered information that would necessitate changes?

165. What are current process problems?

166. How much testing do you need to do to prove that your system is safe?

167. Can the requirement be changed without a large impact on other requirements?

168. What is the risk associated with cost and schedule?

169. What is your Elevator Speech?

170. What will be the integration problems?

171. Is the requirement realistically testable?

2.5 Requirements Traceability Matrix: Microsoft Dynamics 365 For Finance And Operations

172. Will you use a Requirements Traceability Matrix?

173. Why use a WBS?

174. How will it affect the stakeholders personally in career?

175. Describe the process for approving requirements so they can be added to the traceability matrix and Microsoft Dynamics 365 For Finance And Operations project work can be performed. Will the Microsoft Dynamics 365 For Finance And Operations project requirements become approved in writing?

176. How small is small enough?

177. Do you have a clear understanding of all subcontracts in place?

178. Is there a requirements traceability process in place?

179. How do you manage scope?

180. What percentage of Microsoft Dynamics 365 For Finance And Operations projects are producing traceability matrices between requirements and other work products?

181. Why do you manage scope?

182. What is the WBS?

183. What are the chronologies, contingencies, consequences, criteria?

2.6 Project Scope Statement: Microsoft Dynamics 365 For Finance And Operations

184. Risks?

185. What is a process you might recommend to verify the accuracy of the research deliverable?

186. Which risks does the Microsoft Dynamics 365 For Finance And Operations project focus on?

187. Have you been able to thoroughly document the Microsoft Dynamics 365 For Finance And Operations projects assumptions and constraints?

188. Is this process communicated to the customer and team members?

189. Have you been able to easily identify success criteria and create objective measurements for each of the Microsoft Dynamics 365 For Finance And Operations project scopes goal statements?

190. What went right?

191. Are there specific processes you will use to evaluate and approve/reject changes?

192. If the scope changes, what will the impact be to your Microsoft Dynamics 365 For Finance And Operations project in terms of duration, cost, quality, or any other important areas of the Microsoft

Dynamics 365 For Finance And Operations project?

193. Is the change control process documented and on file?

194. What is change?

195. Write a brief purpose statement for this Microsoft Dynamics 365 For Finance And Operations project. Include a business justification statement. What is the product of this Microsoft Dynamics 365 For Finance And Operations project?

196. Will all Microsoft Dynamics 365 For Finance And Operations project issues be unconditionally tracked through the issue resolution process?

197. Will the qa related information be reported regularly as part of the status reporting mechanisms?

198. Will an issue form be in use?

199. Once its defined, what is the stability of the Microsoft Dynamics 365 For Finance And Operations project scope?

200. Were potential customers involved early in the planning process?

201. Is there a baseline plan against which to measure progress?

202. What should you drop in order to add something new?

2.7 Assumption and Constraint Log: Microsoft Dynamics 365 For Finance And Operations

203. How do you design an auditing system?

204. Is the definition of the Microsoft Dynamics 365 For Finance And Operations project scope clear; what needs to be accomplished?

205. Violation trace: why ?

206. Have adequate resources been provided by management to ensure Microsoft Dynamics 365 For Finance And Operations project success?

207. What is positive about the current process?

208. Is the steering committee active in Microsoft Dynamics 365 For Finance And Operations project oversight?

209. What would you gain if you spent time working to improve this process?

210. Should factors be unpredictable over time?

211. What worked well?

212. Has the approach and development strategy of the Microsoft Dynamics 365 For Finance And Operations project been defined, documented and accepted by the appropriate stakeholders?

213. If it is out of compliance, should the process be amended or should the Plan be amended?

214. How can you prevent/fix violations?

215. Are there standards for code development?

216. If appropriate, is the deliverable content consistent with current Microsoft Dynamics 365 For Finance And Operations project documents and in compliance with the Document Management Plan?

217. Have all necessary approvals been obtained?

218. Have all stakeholders been identified?

219. Does the Microsoft Dynamics 365 For Finance And Operations project have a formal Microsoft Dynamics 365 For Finance And Operations project Plan?

220. Has a Microsoft Dynamics 365 For Finance And Operations project Communications Plan been developed?

221. Were the system requirements formally reviewed prior to initiating the design phase?

2.8 Work Breakdown Structure: Microsoft Dynamics 365 For Finance And Operations

222. Who has to do it?

223. Can you make it?

224. Why would you develop a Work Breakdown Structure?

225. When do you stop?

226. What is the probability that the Microsoft Dynamics 365 For Finance And Operations project duration will exceed xx weeks?

227. Do you need another level?

228. How far down?

229. What has to be done?

230. Is it still viable?

231. How many levels?

232. Where does it take place?

233. What is the probability of completing the Microsoft Dynamics 365 For Finance And Operations project in less that xx days?

234. Why is it useful?

235. Is the work breakdown structure (wbs) defined and is the scope of the Microsoft Dynamics 365 For Finance And Operations project clear with assigned deliverable owners?

236. When does it have to be done?

237. How big is a work-package?

238. When would you develop a Work Breakdown Structure?

239. How will you and your Microsoft Dynamics 365 For Finance And Operations project team define the Microsoft Dynamics 365 For Finance And Operations projects scope and work breakdown structure?

2.9 WBS Dictionary: Microsoft Dynamics 365 For Finance And Operations

240. Are internal budgets for authorized, and not priced changes based on the contractors resource plan for accomplishing the work?

241. Are significant decision points, constraints, and interfaces identified as key milestones?

242. Is budgeted cost for work performed calculated in a manner consistent with the way work is planned?

243. Where engineering standards or other internal work measurement systems are used, is there a formal relationship between corresponding values and work package budgets?

244. Does the contractors system identify work accomplishment against the schedule plan?

245. Is cost performance measurement at the point in time most suitable for the category of material involved, and no earlier than the time of actual receipt of material?

246. Does the contractors system provide unit costs, equivalent unit or lot costs in terms of labor, material, other direct, and indirect costs?

247. Is data disseminated to the contractors management timely, accurate, and usable?

248. Are the responsibilities and authorities of each of the above organizational elements or managers clearly defined?

249. Are direct or indirect cost adjustments being accomplished according to accounting procedures acceptable to us?

250. Are data elements (BCWS, BCWP, and ACWP) progressively summarized from the detail level to the contract level through the CWBS?

251. Are all elements of indirect expense identified to overhead cost budgets of Microsoft Dynamics 365 For Finance And Operations projections?

252. The Microsoft Dynamics 365 For Finance And Operations projected business base for each period?

253. Performance to date and material commitment?

254. Are the procedures for identifying indirect costs to incurring organizations, indirect cost pools, and allocating the costs from the pools to the contracts formally documented?

255. Are estimates of costs at completion utilized in determining contract funding requirements and reporting them?

256. Identify potential or actual overruns and underruns?

257. Does the scheduling system identify in a timely manner the status of work?

258. Knowledgeable Microsoft Dynamics 365 For Finance And Operations projections of future performance?

259. Is the work done on a work package level as described in the WBS dictionary?

2.10 Schedule Management Plan: Microsoft Dynamics 365 For Finance And Operations

260. Has a sponsor been identified?

261. Define units of measurement for each resource. For example, are you referencing gallons or liters?

262. Were stakeholders aware and supportive of the principles and practices of modern software estimation?

263. Are actuals compared against estimates to analyze and correct variances?

264. Have stakeholder accountabilities & responsibilities been clearly defined?

265. Does the Microsoft Dynamics 365 For Finance And Operations project have a formal Microsoft Dynamics 365 For Finance And Operations project Charter?

266. Does the ims reflect accurate current status and credible start/finish forecasts for all to-go tasks and milestones?

267. Are cause and effect determined for risks when they occur?

268. Are vendor invoices audited for accuracy before payment?

269. Is your organization certified as a supplier, wholesaler and/or regular dealer?

270. Are corrective actions and variances reported?

271. Are tasks tracked by hours?

272. Have the key elements of a coherent Microsoft Dynamics 365 For Finance And Operations project management strategy been established?

273. Is a payment system in place with proper reviews and approvals?

274. Are all activities logically sequenced?

275. Have the key functions and capabilities been defined and assigned to each release or iteration?

276. Are changes in deliverable commitments agreed to by all affected groups & individuals?

277. Will the Microsoft Dynamics 365 For Finance And Operations project sponsor be involved in preliminary schedule reviews?

2.11 Activity List: Microsoft Dynamics 365 For Finance And Operations

278. Who will perform the work?

279. Is infrastructure setup part of your Microsoft Dynamics 365 For Finance And Operations project?

280. When do the individual activities need to start and finish?

281. What is the LF and LS for each activity?

282. Where will it be performed?

283. What will be performed?

284. What are you counting on?

285. What went wrong?

286. How can the Microsoft Dynamics 365 For Finance And Operations project be displayed graphically to better visualize the activities?

287. What is the total time required to complete the Microsoft Dynamics 365 For Finance And Operations project if no delays occur?

288. When will the work be performed?

289. How should ongoing costs be monitored to try to keep the Microsoft Dynamics 365 For Finance And

Operations project within budget?

290. How do you determine the late start (LS) for each activity?

291. What is the probability the Microsoft Dynamics 365 For Finance And Operations project can be completed in xx weeks?

292. What is your organizations history in doing similar activities?

293. What are the critical bottleneck activities?

294. How will it be performed?

295. Are the required resources available or need to be acquired?

2.12 Activity Attributes: Microsoft Dynamics 365 For Finance And Operations

296. Activity: fair or not fair?

297. How much activity detail is required?

298. Is there anything planned that does not need to be here?

299. Does your organization of the data change its meaning?

300. Are the required resources available?

301. Why?

302. What is missing?

303. How difficult will it be to do specific activities on this Microsoft Dynamics 365 For Finance And Operations project?

304. Activity: what is Missing?

305. What conclusions/generalizations can you draw from this?

306. What activity do you think you should spend the most time on?

307. Has management defined a definite timeframe

for the turnaround or Microsoft Dynamics 365 For Finance And Operations project window?

308. Have constraints been applied to the start and finish milestones for the phases?

309. Do you feel very comfortable with your prediction?

310. Were there other ways you could have organized the data to achieve similar results?

311. How do you manage time?

312. Activity: what is In the Bag?

2.13 Milestone List: Microsoft Dynamics 365 For Finance And Operations

313. Sustainable financial backing?

314. When will the Microsoft Dynamics 365 For Finance And Operations project be complete?

315. What is the market for your technology, product or service?

316. How late can each activity be finished and started?

317. Usps (unique selling points)?

318. Gaps in capabilities?

319. How late can the activity finish?

320. What has been done so far?

321. Milestone pages should display the UserID of the person who added the milestone. Does a report or query exist that provides this audit information?

322. Competitive advantages?

323. Environmental effects?

324. Identify critical paths (one or more) and which activities are on the critical path?

325. Obstacles faced?

326. Insurmountable weaknesses?

327. Describe the concept of the technology, product or service that will be or has been developed. How will it be used?

328. Political effects?

329. Describe your organizations strengths and core competencies. What factors will make your organization succeed?

2.14 Network Diagram: Microsoft Dynamics 365 For Finance And Operations

330. If a current contract exists, can you provide the vendor name, contract start, and contract expiration date?

331. Are the gantt chart and/or network diagram updated periodically and used to assess the overall Microsoft Dynamics 365 For Finance And Operations project timetable?

332. Will crashing x weeks return more in benefits than it costs?

333. What controls the start and finish of a job?

334. What to do and When?

335. What is the completion time?

336. Exercise: what is the probability that the Microsoft Dynamics 365 For Finance And Operations project duration will exceed xx weeks?

337. What activities must follow this activity?

338. Are you on time?

339. How confident can you be in your milestone dates and the delivery date?

340. Where do you schedule uncertainty time?

341. What are the Key Success Factors?

342. Which type of network diagram allows you to depict four types of dependencies?

343. What job or jobs could run concurrently?

344. What are the tools?

345. What job or jobs precede it?

346. What must be completed before an activity can be started?

347. What is the probability of completing the Microsoft Dynamics 365 For Finance And Operations project in less that xx days?

348. What is the lowest cost to complete this Microsoft Dynamics 365 For Finance And Operations project in xx weeks?

2.15 Activity Resource Requirements: Microsoft Dynamics 365 For Finance And Operations

349. Other support in specific areas?

350. What is the Work Plan Standard?

351. Are there unresolved issues that need to be addressed?

352. Organizational Applicability?

353. Why do you do that?

354. How do you handle petty cash?

355. Which logical relationship does the PDM use most often?

356. What are constraints that you might find during the Human Resource Planning process?

357. Time for overtime?

358. Do you use tools like decomposition and rolling-wave planning to produce the activity list and other outputs?

359. When does monitoring begin?

360. Anything else?

361. How many signatures do you require on a check and does this match what is in your policy and procedures?

2.16 Resource Breakdown Structure: Microsoft Dynamics 365 For Finance And Operations

362. What is the difference between % Complete and % work?

363. What is the primary purpose of the human resource plan?

364. Who will use the system?

365. What is Microsoft Dynamics 365 For Finance And Operations project communication management?

366. Who is allowed to perform which functions?

367. Is predictive resource analysis being done?

368. Who needs what information?

369. Why is this important?

370. What is each stakeholders desired outcome for the Microsoft Dynamics 365 For Finance And Operations project?

371. Changes based on input from stakeholders?

372. Who is allowed to see what data about which resources?

373. What is the purpose of assigning and

documenting responsibility?

374. When do they need the information?

375. What defines a successful Microsoft Dynamics 365 For Finance And Operations project?

376. How can this help you with team building?

377. Who delivers the information?

2.17 Activity Duration Estimates: Microsoft Dynamics 365 For Finance And Operations

378. What are the main types of contracts if you do decide to outsource?

379. What is wrong with this scenario?

380. What questions do you have about the sample documents provided?

381. Are performance reviews conducted regularly to assess the status of Microsoft Dynamics 365 For Finance And Operations projects?

382. What is involved in the solicitation process?

383. Is earned value analysis completed to assess Microsoft Dynamics 365 For Finance And Operations project performance?

384. What distinguishes one organization from another in this area?

385. Are adjustments implemented to correct or prevent defects?

386. What do corresponding sources say about Microsoft Dynamics 365 For Finance And Operations project management?

387. Find an example of a contract for information

technology services. Analyze the key features of the contract. What type of contract was used and why?

388. What is the career outlook for Microsoft Dynamics 365 For Finance And Operations project managers in information technology?

389. On which process should team members spend the most time?

390. Who has the PRIMARY responsibility to solve this problem?

391. Which frame seemed to be the most important and why?

392. Do you agree with the suggestions provided for improving Microsoft Dynamics 365 For Finance And Operations project communications?

393. How do you enter durations, link tasks, and view critical path information?

394. If you plan to take the PMP exam soon, what should you do to prepare?

395. Are changes to the scope managed according to defined procedures?

2.18 Duration Estimating Worksheet: Microsoft Dynamics 365 For Finance And Operations

396. Why estimate costs?

397. When, then?

398. Can the Microsoft Dynamics 365 For Finance And Operations project be constructed as planned?

399. What is an Average Microsoft Dynamics 365 For Finance And Operations project?

400. What utility impacts are there?

401. Does the Microsoft Dynamics 365 For Finance And Operations project provide innovative ways for stakeholders to overcome obstacles or deliver better outcomes?

402. What is your role?

403. For other activities, how much delay can be tolerated?

404. What info is needed?

405. What is cost and Microsoft Dynamics 365 For Finance And Operations project cost management?

406. Small or large Microsoft Dynamics 365 For Finance And Operations project?

407. How should ongoing costs be monitored to try to keep the Microsoft Dynamics 365 For Finance And Operations project within budget?

408. Is this operation cost effective?

409. What is the total time required to complete the Microsoft Dynamics 365 For Finance And Operations project if no delays occur?

410. What questions do you have?

411. Define the work as completely as possible. What work will be included in the Microsoft Dynamics 365 For Finance And Operations project?

412. Done before proceeding with this activity or what can be done concurrently?

413. What is next?

414. Will the Microsoft Dynamics 365 For Finance And Operations project collaborate with the local community and leverage resources?

2.19 Project Schedule: Microsoft Dynamics 365 For Finance And Operations

415. How do you know that youhave done this right?

416. Does the condition or event threaten the Microsoft Dynamics 365 For Finance And Operations projects objectives in any ways?

417. Meet requirements?

418. If you can not fix it, how do you do it differently?

419. How much detail?

420. How can you address that situation?

421. What is Microsoft Dynamics 365 For Finance And Operations project management?

422. Are there activities that came from a template or previous Microsoft Dynamics 365 For Finance And Operations project that are not applicable on this phase of this Microsoft Dynamics 365 For Finance And Operations project?

423. Activity charts and bar charts are graphical representations of a Microsoft Dynamics 365 For Finance And Operations project schedule ...how do they differ?

424. Are the original Microsoft Dynamics 365 For

Finance And Operations project schedule and budget realistic?

425. How can slack be negative?

426. Have all Microsoft Dynamics 365 For Finance And Operations project delays been adequately accounted for, communicated to all stakeholders and adjustments made in overall Microsoft Dynamics 365 For Finance And Operations project schedule?

427. Why is software Microsoft Dynamics 365 For Finance And Operations project disaster so common?

428. Is Microsoft Dynamics 365 For Finance And Operations project work proceeding in accordance with the original Microsoft Dynamics 365 For Finance And Operations project schedule?

429. How much slack is available in the Microsoft Dynamics 365 For Finance And Operations project?

430. Did the Microsoft Dynamics 365 For Finance And Operations project come in under budget?

431. Schedule/cost recovery?

432. Why do you need schedules?

433. Verify that the update is accurate. Are all remaining durations correct?

2.20 Cost Management Plan: Microsoft Dynamics 365 For Finance And Operations

434. Is the steering committee active in Microsoft Dynamics 365 For Finance And Operations project oversight?

435. Is an industry recognized mechanized support tool(s) being used for Microsoft Dynamics 365 For Finance And Operations project scheduling & tracking?

436. Are quality inspections and review activities listed in the Microsoft Dynamics 365 For Finance And Operations project schedule(s)?

437. How relevant is this attribute to this Microsoft Dynamics 365 For Finance And Operations project or audit?

438. Estimating responsibilities – how will the responsibilities for cost estimating be allocated?

439. What is the work breakdown structure for the Microsoft Dynamics 365 For Finance And Operations project?

440. Is a pmo (Microsoft Dynamics 365 For Finance And Operations project management office) in place and provide oversight to the Microsoft Dynamics 365 For Finance And Operations project?

441. Why do you manage cost?

442. Are written status reports provided on a designated frequent basis?

443. Is your organization certified as a broker of the products/supplies?

444. What does this mean to a cost or scheduler manager?

445. Is it a Microsoft Dynamics 365 For Finance And Operations project?

446. Is there any form of automated support for Issues Management?

447. Are all key components of a Quality Assurance Plan present?

448. Technical and functional?

449. Contingency rundown curve be used on the Microsoft Dynamics 365 For Finance And Operations project?

450. Owner, contractor, and subcontractors?

451. Has a Microsoft Dynamics 365 For Finance And Operations project Communications Plan been developed?

452. Are the key elements of a Microsoft Dynamics 365 For Finance And Operations project Charter present?

2.21 Activity Cost Estimates: Microsoft Dynamics 365 For Finance And Operations

453. Were you satisfied with the work?

454. How do you fund change orders?

455. Maintenance Reserve?

456. Where can you get activity reports?

457. What were things that you did well, and could improve, and how?

458. What is your organizations history in doing similar tasks?

459. One way to define activities is to consider how organization employees describe jobs to families and friends. You basically want to know, What do you do?

460. What makes a good expected result statement?

461. Can you change your activities?

462. Who & what determines the need for contracted services?

463. Would you hire them again?

464. Can you delete activities or make them inactive?

465. What is the last item a Microsoft Dynamics 365 For Finance And Operations project manager must do to finalize Microsoft Dynamics 365 For Finance And Operations project close-out?

466. If you are asked to lower your estimate because the price is too high, what are your options?

467. How difficult will it be to do specific tasks on the Microsoft Dynamics 365 For Finance And Operations project?

468. Is there anything unique in this Microsoft Dynamics 365 For Finance And Operations projects scope statement that will affect resources?

469. What is the activity inventory?

470. Does the activity use a common approach or business function to deliver its results?

2.22 Cost Estimating Worksheet: Microsoft Dynamics 365 For Finance And Operations

471. What additional Microsoft Dynamics 365 For Finance And Operations project(s) could be initiated as a result of this Microsoft Dynamics 365 For Finance And Operations project?

472. Does the Microsoft Dynamics 365 For Finance And Operations project provide innovative ways for stakeholders to overcome obstacles or deliver better outcomes?

473. Is it feasible to establish a control group arrangement?

474. What can be included?

475. What happens to any remaining funds not used?

476. What costs are to be estimated?

477. What is the purpose of estimating?

478. Will the Microsoft Dynamics 365 For Finance And Operations project collaborate with the local community and leverage resources?

479. How will the results be shared and to whom?

480. What is the estimated labor cost today based upon this information?

481. What will others want?

482. Identify the timeframe necessary to monitor progress and collect data to determine how the selected measure has changed?

483. Ask: are others positioned to know, are others credible, and will others cooperate?

484. Value pocket identification & quantification what are value pockets?

485. Can a trend be established from historical performance data on the selected measure and are the criteria for using trend analysis or forecasting methods met?

486. Who is best positioned to know and assist in identifying corresponding factors?

487. Is the Microsoft Dynamics 365 For Finance And Operations project responsive to community need?

2.23 Cost Baseline: Microsoft Dynamics 365 For Finance And Operations

488. Is request in line with priorities?

489. Has the actual cost of the Microsoft Dynamics 365 For Finance And Operations project (or Microsoft Dynamics 365 For Finance And Operations project phase) been tallied and compared to the approved budget?

490. Have all approved changes to the Microsoft Dynamics 365 For Finance And Operations project requirement been identified and impact on the performance, cost, and schedule baselines documented?

491. On time?

492. How accurate do cost estimates need to be?

493. Has the documentation relating to operation and maintenance of the product(s) or service(s) been delivered to, and accepted by, operations management?

494. What deliverables come first?

495. Is the requested change request a result of changes in other Microsoft Dynamics 365 For Finance And Operations project(s)?

496. What would the life cycle costs be?

497. Are procedures defined by which the cost baseline may be changed?

498. Does the suggested change request represent a desired enhancement to the products functionality?

499. How long are you willing to wait before you find out were late?

500. What is it ?

501. How fast?

502. Has training and knowledge transfer of the operations organization been completed?

503. Eac -estimate at completion, what is the total job expected to cost?

504. Vac -variance at completion, how much over/ under budget do you expect to be?

2.24 Quality Management Plan: Microsoft Dynamics 365 For Finance And Operations

505. Modifications to the requirements?

506. What procedures are used to determine if you use, and the number of split, replicate or duplicate samples taken at a site?

507. How are changes recorded?

508. How does your organization determine the requirements and product/service features important to customers?

509. Are requirements management tracking tools and procedures in place?

510. How does your organization design processes to ensure others meet customer and others requirements?

511. Are there trends or hot spots?

512. How are people conducting sampling trained?

513. Are qmps good forever?

514. How are senior leaders, employees, and your organization involved in supporting the community?

515. Where do you focus?

516. Is it necessary?

517. How do you ensure that your sampling methods and procedures meet your data quality objectives?

518. Are there nonconformance issues?

519. How effectively was the Quality Management Plan applied during Microsoft Dynamics 365 For Finance And Operations project Execution?

520. You know what your customers expectations are regarding this process?

521. How does your organization decide what to measure?

522. How many Microsoft Dynamics 365 For Finance And Operations project staff does this specific process affect?

523. What else should you do now?

524. How are changes to procedures made?

2.25 Quality Metrics: Microsoft Dynamics 365 For Finance And Operations

525. What forces exist that would cause them to change?

526. Where did complaints, returns and warranty claims come from?

527. How should customers provide input?

528. Was material distributed on time?

529. What are you trying to accomplish?

530. Has trace of defects been initiated?

531. If the defect rate during testing is substantially higher than that of the previous release (or a similar product), then ask: Did you plan for and actually improve testing effectiveness?

532. How do you calculate such metrics?

533. What metrics do you measure?

534. Why is now the time for quality metrics?

535. Which report did you use to create the data you are submitting?

536. What are your organizations next steps?

537. What documentation is required?

538. Is material complete (and does it meet the standards)?

539. What can manufacturing professionals do to ensure quality is seen as an integral part of the entire product lifecycle?

540. Are quality metrics defined?

541. Have risk areas been identified?

542. What happens if you get an abnormal result?

543. What percentage are outcome-based?

544. Can visual measures help you to filter visualizations of interest?

2.26 Process Improvement Plan: Microsoft Dynamics 365 For Finance And Operations

545. Have the supporting tools been developed or acquired?

546. What is the return on investment?

547. How do you manage quality?

548. Have the frequency of collection and the points in the process where measurements will be made been determined?

549. What personnel are the champions for the initiative?

550. What makes people good SPI coaches?

551. Are you meeting the quality standards?

552. The motive is determined by asking, Why do you want to achieve this goal?

553. Why do you want to achieve the goal?

554. What lessons have you learned so far?

555. Where do you want to be?

556. Are you making progress on the improvement framework?

557. Does your process ensure quality?

558. Are there forms and procedures to collect and record the data?

559. What actions are needed to address the problems and achieve the goals?

560. Has a process guide to collect the data been developed?

561. To elicit goal statements, do you ask a question such as, What do you want to achieve?

562. Why quality management?

2.27 Responsibility Assignment Matrix: Microsoft Dynamics 365 For Finance And Operations

563. What tool can show you individual and group allocations?

564. What is the number one predictor of a groups productivity?

565. Changes in the current direct and Microsoft Dynamics 365 For Finance And Operations projected base?

566. Are all authorized tasks assigned to identified organizational elements?

567. Microsoft Dynamics 365 For Finance And Operations projected economic escalation?

568. How cost benefit analysis?

569. What are some important Microsoft Dynamics 365 For Finance And Operations project communications management tools?

570. Does the contractor use objective results, design reviews and tests to trace schedule performance?

571. Contemplated overhead expenditure for each period based on the best information currently available?

572. Are control accounts opened and closed based on the start and completion of work contained therein?

573. The already stated responsible for overhead performance control of related costs?

574. Are too many reports done in writing instead of verbally?

575. Wbs elements contractually specified for reporting of status (lowest level only)?

576. Budgeted cost for work performed?

577. What do you do when people do not respond?

578. Are overhead costs budgets established on a basis consistent with anticipated direct business base?

579. Is every signing-off responsibility and every communicating responsibility critically necessary?

2.28 Roles and Responsibilities: Microsoft Dynamics 365 For Finance And Operations

580. Where are you most strong as a supervisor?

581. Attainable / achievable: the goal is attainable; can you actually accomplish the goal?

582. Does the team have access to and ability to use data analysis tools?

583. What expectations were NOT met?

584. What expectations were met?

585. Who is involved?

586. Authority: what areas/Microsoft Dynamics 365 For Finance And Operations projects in your work do you have the authority to decide upon and act on the already stated decisions?

587. Do you take the time to clearly define roles and responsibilities on Microsoft Dynamics 365 For Finance And Operations project tasks?

588. Are your policies supportive of a culture of quality data?

589. Are your budgets supportive of a culture of quality data?

590. Accountabilities: what are the roles and responsibilities of individual team members?

591. Are governance roles and responsibilities documented?

592. What is working well within your organizations performance management system?

593. To decide whether to use a quality measurement, ask how will you know when it is achieved?

594. What should you do now to ensure that you are meeting all expectations of your current position?

595. Required skills, knowledge, experience?

596. Was the expectation clearly communicated?

597. Key conclusions and recommendations: Are conclusions and recommendations relevant and acceptable?

598. What should you highlight for improvement?

2.29 Human Resource Management Plan: Microsoft Dynamics 365 For Finance And Operations

599. Were Microsoft Dynamics 365 For Finance And Operations project team members involved in detailed estimating and scheduling?

600. Are quality inspections and review activities listed in the Microsoft Dynamics 365 For Finance And Operations project schedule(s)?

601. Are parking lot items captured?

602. Is your organization primarily focused on a specific industry?

603. What talent is needed?

604. Has a resource management plan been created?

605. Have all unresolved risks been documented?

606. Does the Microsoft Dynamics 365 For Finance And Operations project have a Quality Culture?

607. Is there a set of procedures defining the scope, procedures, and deliverables defining quality control?

608. Is the communication plan being followed?

609. Are Microsoft Dynamics 365 For Finance And Operations project team members involved in

detailed estimating and scheduling?

610. Are status reports received per the Microsoft Dynamics 365 For Finance And Operations project Plan?

611. Has your organization readiness assessment been conducted?

612. What were things that you need to improve?

613. Microsoft Dynamics 365 For Finance And Operations project definition & scope?

614. Is there an onboarding process in place?

615. Are software metrics formally captured, analyzed and used as a basis for other Microsoft Dynamics 365 For Finance And Operations project estimates?

616. How are you going to ensure that you have a well motivated workforce?

617. Is your organization certified as a supplier, wholesaler, regular dealer, or manufacturer of corresponding products/supplies?

2.30 Communications Management Plan: Microsoft Dynamics 365 For Finance And Operations

618. Do you feel more overwhelmed by stakeholders?

619. Timing: when do the effects of the communication take place?

620. What to learn?

621. Who needs to know and how much?

622. Who to share with?

623. Who to learn from?

624. Which stakeholders are thought leaders, influences, or early adopters?

625. Are there too many who have an interest in some aspect of your work?

626. Do you ask; can you recommend others for you to talk with about this initiative?

627. Are there common objectives between the team and the stakeholder?

628. Who are the members of the governing body?

629. Who is involved as you identify stakeholders?

630. What steps can you take for a positive relationship?

631. Conflict resolution -which method when?

632. What is the stakeholders level of authority?

633. Who did you turn to if you had questions?

634. Who were proponents/opponents?

635. In your work, how much time is spent on stakeholder identification?

636. How often do you engage with stakeholders?

2.31 Risk Management Plan: Microsoft Dynamics 365 For Finance And Operations

637. User involvement: do you have the right users?

638. Should the risk be taken at all?

639. Do you have a consistent repeatable process that is actually used?

640. Technology risk: is the Microsoft Dynamics 365 For Finance And Operations project technically feasible?

641. Are the required plans included, such as nonstructural flood risk management plans?

642. What is the likelihood?

643. Where are you confronted with risks during the business phases?

644. Mitigation -how can you avoid the risk?

645. What are some questions that should be addressed in a risk management plan?

646. For software; are compilers and code generators available and suitable for the product to be built?

647. Why do you need to manage Microsoft Dynamics 365 For Finance And Operations project Risk?

648. How quickly does this item need to be resolved?

649. Was an original risk assessment/risk management plan completed?

650. Which is an input to the risk management process?

651. What are the cost, schedule and resource impacts of avoiding the risk?

652. Market risk: will the new product be useful to your organization or marketable to others?

653. Can the risk be avoided by choosing a different alternative?

654. Are the participants able to keep up with the workload?

2.32 Risk Register: Microsoft Dynamics 365 For Finance And Operations

655. How well are risks controlled?

656. What are the main aims, objectives of the policy, strategy, or service and the intended outcomes?

657. What are your key risks/show istoppers and what is being done to manage them?

658. What is the probability and impact of the risk occurring?

659. Market risk -will the new service or product be useful to your organization or marketable to others?

660. Who needs to know about this?

661. Are there other alternative controls that could be implemented?

662. What may happen or not go according to plan?

663. Manageability – have mitigations to the risk been identified?

664. What risks might negatively or positively affect achieving the Microsoft Dynamics 365 For Finance And Operations project objectives?

665. Amongst the action plans and recommendations

that you have to introduce are there some that could stop or delay the overall program?

666. What is your current and future risk profile?

667. Have other controls and solutions been implemented in other services which could be applied as an alternative to additional funding?

668. What can be done about it?

669. What evidence do you have to justify the likelihood score of the risk (audit, incident report, claim, complaints, inspection, internal review)?

670. How often will the Risk Management Plan and Risk Register be formally reviewed, and by whom?

671. What has changed since the last period?

672. What is the appropriate level of risk management for this Microsoft Dynamics 365 For Finance And Operations project?

673. What further options might be available for responding to the risk?

2.33 Probability and Impact Assessment: Microsoft Dynamics 365 For Finance And Operations

674. Who should be notified of the occurrence of each of the risk indicators?

675. Would avoiding any of corresponding impact the Microsoft Dynamics 365 For Finance And Operations projects chance of success?

676. What will be cost of redeployment of personnel?

677. What are your data sources?

678. How risk averse are you?

679. Are testing tools available and suitable?

680. What is the likelihood of a breakthrough?

681. Monitoring of the overall Microsoft Dynamics 365 For Finance And Operations project status – are there any changes in the Microsoft Dynamics 365 For Finance And Operations project that can effect and cause new possible risks?

682. How do you define a risk?

683. Do requirements demand the use of new analysis, design, or testing methods?

684. Are trained personnel, including supervisors and

Microsoft Dynamics 365 For Finance And Operations project managers, available to handle such a large Microsoft Dynamics 365 For Finance And Operations project?

685. Sensitivity analysis -which risks will have the most impact on the Microsoft Dynamics 365 For Finance And Operations project?

686. Have customers been involved fully in the definition of requirements?

687. How do risks change during the Microsoft Dynamics 365 For Finance And Operations projects life cycle?

688. Is it necessary to deeply assess all Microsoft Dynamics 365 For Finance And Operations project risks?

689. What risks are necessary to achieve success?

690. Do you have specific methods that you use for each phase of the process?

691. How completely has the customer been identified?

692. Do requirements put excessive performance constraints on the product?

693. Does the software engineering team have the right mix of skills?

2.34 Probability and Impact Matrix: Microsoft Dynamics 365 For Finance And Operations

694. Are you on schedule?

695. Can the Microsoft Dynamics 365 For Finance And Operations project proceed without assuming the risk?

696. Have you worked with the customer in the past?

697. What are the ways you measure and evaluate risks?

698. Are there new risks that mitigation strategies might introduce?

699. Does the customer understand the software process?

700. Were there any Microsoft Dynamics 365 For Finance And Operations projects similar to this one in existence?

701. What things might go wrong?

702. What are the chances the risk events will occur?

703. What are the likely future requirements?

704. Several experts are offsite, and wish to be included. How can this be done?

705. Can it be enlarged by drawing people from other areas of your organization?

706. Are some people working on multiple Microsoft Dynamics 365 For Finance And Operations projects?

707. How do risks change during the Microsoft Dynamics 365 For Finance And Operations projects life cycle?

708. Are people attending meetings and doing work?

709. Amount of reused software?

710. How realistic is the timing of introduction?

711. Premium on reliability of product?

712. How is the Microsoft Dynamics 365 For Finance And Operations project going to be managed?

2.35 Risk Data Sheet: Microsoft Dynamics 365 For Finance And Operations

713. What are you trying to achieve (Objectives)?

714. During work activities could hazards exist?

715. What were the Causes that contributed?

716. Has a sensitivity analysis been carried out?

717. What is the environment within which you operate (social trends, economic, community values, broad based participation, national directions etc.)?

718. Do effective diagnostic tests exist?

719. Who has a vested interest in how you perform as your organization (our stakeholders)?

720. How reliable is the data source?

721. What are the main threats to your existence?

722. If it happens, what are the consequences?

723. What can happen?

724. What actions can be taken to eliminate or remove risk?

725. What is the chance that it will happen?

726. How can hazards be reduced?

727. What do people affected think about the need for, and practicality of preventive measures?

728. Are new hazards created?

729. How can it happen?

730. What are the main opportunities available to you that you should grab while you can?

2.36 Procurement Management Plan: Microsoft Dynamics 365 For Finance And Operations

731. Is there a formal set of procedures supporting Issues Management?

732. How will multiple providers be managed?

733. Are Microsoft Dynamics 365 For Finance And Operations project leaders committed to this Microsoft Dynamics 365 For Finance And Operations project full time?

734. Are the payment terms being followed?

735. Does the detailed work plan match the complexity of tasks with the capabilities of personnel?

736. Does the Microsoft Dynamics 365 For Finance And Operations project have a Quality Culture?

737. Have lessons learned been conducted after each Microsoft Dynamics 365 For Finance And Operations project release?

738. Are any non-compliance issues that exist communicated to your organization?

739. Are the appropriate IT resources adequate to meet planned commitments?

740. Is the schedule updated on a periodic basis?

741. Are the results of quality assurance reviews provided to affected groups & individuals?

742. Why is procurement planning important?

743. Do all stakeholders know how to access the PM repository and where to find the Microsoft Dynamics 365 For Finance And Operations project documentation?

744. Is the Microsoft Dynamics 365 For Finance And Operations project sponsor clearly communicating the business case or rationale for why this Microsoft Dynamics 365 For Finance And Operations project is needed?

745. Are estimating assumptions and constraints captured?

746. Alignment to strategic goals & objectives?

747. Have adequate resources been provided by management to ensure Microsoft Dynamics 365 For Finance And Operations project success?

748. Is the quality assurance team identified?

2.37 Source Selection Criteria: Microsoft Dynamics 365 For Finance And Operations

749. Can you reasonably estimate total organization requirements for the coming year?

750. Is a cost realism analysis used?

751. Team leads: what is your process for assigning ratings?

752. How do you facilitate evaluation against published criteria?

753. Is the contracting office likely to receive more purchase requests for this item or service during the coming year?

754. What documentation should be used to support the selection decision?

755. In the technical/management area, what criteria do you use to determine the final evaluation ratings?

756. Are resultant proposal revisions allowed?

757. What should be the contracting officers strategy?

758. When and what information can be considered with offerors regarding past performance?

759. Does the evaluation of any change include an

impact analysis; how will the change affect the scope, time, cost, and quality of the goods or services being provided?

760. What does an evaluation address and what does a sample resemble?

761. How should the preproposal conference be conducted?

762. In order of importance, which evaluation criteria are the most critical to the determination of your overall rating?

763. What should communications be used to accomplish?

764. Can you make a cost/technical tradeoff?

765. What risks were identified in the proposals?

766. What are the most common types of rating systems?

767. How much weight should be placed on past performance information?

2.38 Stakeholder Management Plan: Microsoft Dynamics 365 For Finance And Operations

768. Have Microsoft Dynamics 365 For Finance And Operations project success criteria been defined?

769. Is Microsoft Dynamics 365 For Finance And Operations project status reviewed with the steering and executive teams at appropriate intervals?

770. Are stakeholders aware and supportive of the principles and practices of modern software estimation?

771. Does the Microsoft Dynamics 365 For Finance And Operations project have a formal Microsoft Dynamics 365 For Finance And Operations project Plan?

772. What methods are to be used for managing and monitoring subcontractors (eg agreements, contracts etc)?

773. What specific resources will be required for implementation activities?

774. Are there procedures in place to effectively manage interdependencies with other Microsoft Dynamics 365 For Finance And Operations projects / systems?

775. Which risks pose the highest threat?

776. How much information should be collected?

777. Do you use diagrams and tables to account for complex concepts and increase overall readability?

778. Have Microsoft Dynamics 365 For Finance And Operations project success criteria been defined?

779. What is the difference between product and Microsoft Dynamics 365 For Finance And Operations project scope?

780. When would you develop a Microsoft Dynamics 365 For Finance And Operations project Business Plan?

781. Does the Microsoft Dynamics 365 For Finance And Operations project have a formal Microsoft Dynamics 365 For Finance And Operations project Charter?

782. How are the overall Microsoft Dynamics 365 For Finance And Operations project development processes to be undertaken to produce the Microsoft Dynamics 365 For Finance And Operations project outputs?

783. Has the schedule been baselined?

784. Are decisions captured in a decisions log?

2.39 Change Management Plan: Microsoft Dynamics 365 For Finance And Operations

785. Who will be the change levers?

786. What do you expect the target audience to do, say, think or feel as a result of this communication?

787. What can you do to minimise misinterpretation and negative perceptions?

788. Are work location changes required?

789. What goal(s) do you hope to accomplish?

790. How frequently should you repeat the message?

791. What processes are in place to manage knowledge about the Microsoft Dynamics 365 For Finance And Operations project?

792. What communication network would you use – informal or formal?

793. What are the responsibilities assigned to each role?

794. Is there an adequate supply of people for the new roles?

795. Readiness -what is a successful end state?

796. What risks may occur upfront?

797. What are the specific target groups/audiences that will be impacted by this change?

798. Has a training need analysis been carried out?

799. When does it make sense to customize?

800. Will the readiness criteria be met prior to the training roll out?

801. What are you trying to achieve as a result of communication?

802. When should a given message be communicated?

803. What are the specific target groups / audience that will be impacted by this change?

3.0 Executing Process Group: Microsoft Dynamics 365 For Finance And Operations

804. What were things that you did very well and want to do the same again on the next Microsoft Dynamics 365 For Finance And Operations project?

805. In what way has the program come up with innovative measures for problem-solving?

806. How can software assist in Microsoft Dynamics 365 For Finance And Operations project communications?

807. What are the challenges Microsoft Dynamics 365 For Finance And Operations project teams face?

808. Does the Microsoft Dynamics 365 For Finance And Operations project team have enough people to execute the Microsoft Dynamics 365 For Finance And Operations project plan?

809. What are the Microsoft Dynamics 365 For Finance And Operations project management deliverables of each process group?

810. Do schedule issues conflicts?

811. Could a new application negatively affect the current IT infrastructure?

812. What Microsoft Dynamics 365 For Finance And

Operations projects and services are in the portfolio of your organization?

813. How many different communication channels does the Microsoft Dynamics 365 For Finance And Operations project team have?

814. How is Microsoft Dynamics 365 For Finance And Operations project performance information created and distributed?

815. Who are the Microsoft Dynamics 365 For Finance And Operations project stakeholders?

816. What are deliverables of your Microsoft Dynamics 365 For Finance And Operations project?

817. How do you prevent staff are just doing busywork to pass the time?

818. Specific - is the objective clear in terms of what, how, when, and where the situation will be changed?

819. What does it mean to take a systems view of a Microsoft Dynamics 365 For Finance And Operations project?

820. What are deliverables of your Microsoft Dynamics 365 For Finance And Operations project?

821. Would you rate yourself as being risk-averse, risk-neutral, or risk-seeking?

822. What is the product of your Microsoft Dynamics 365 For Finance And Operations project?

3.1 Team Member Status Report: Microsoft Dynamics 365 For Finance And Operations

823. Does your organization have the means (staff, money, contract, etc.) to produce or to acquire the product, good, or service?

824. What is to be done?

825. Will the staff do training or is that done by a third party?

826. Does the product, good, or service already exist within your organization?

827. Are the products of your organizations Microsoft Dynamics 365 For Finance And Operations projects meeting customers objectives?

828. Are your organizations Microsoft Dynamics 365 For Finance And Operations projects more successful over time?

829. How does this product, good, or service meet the needs of the Microsoft Dynamics 365 For Finance And Operations project and your organization as a whole?

830. How can you make it practical?

831. Do you have an Enterprise Microsoft Dynamics 365 For Finance And Operations project Management Office (EPMO)?

832. Are the attitudes of staff regarding Microsoft Dynamics 365 For Finance And Operations project work improving?

833. How it is to be done?

834. Is there evidence that staff is taking a more professional approach toward management of your organizations Microsoft Dynamics 365 For Finance And Operations projects?

835. Why is it to be done?

836. How will resource planning be done?

837. How much risk is involved?

838. What specific interest groups do you have in place?

839. Does every department have to have a Microsoft Dynamics 365 For Finance And Operations project Manager on staff?

840. When a teams productivity and success depend on collaboration and the efficient flow of information, what generally fails them?

841. The problem with Reward & Recognition Programs is that the truly deserving people all too often get left out. How can you make it practical?

3.2 Change Request: Microsoft Dynamics 365 For Finance And Operations

842. What are the Impacts to your organization?

843. Who is responsible for the implementation and monitoring of all measures?

844. Which requirements attributes affect the risk to reliability the most?

845. How are the measures for carrying out the change established?

846. Does the schedule include Microsoft Dynamics 365 For Finance And Operations project management time and change request analysis time?

847. Has your address changed?

848. Will there be a change request form in use?

849. Is it feasible to use requirements attributes as predictors of reliability?

850. How to get changes (code) out in a timely manner?

851. For which areas does this operating procedure apply?

852. Who needs to approve change requests?

853. Will all change requests and current status be logged?

854. What mechanism is used to appraise others of changes that are made?

855. Should staff call into the helpdesk or go to the website?

856. Customer acceptance plan how will the customer verify the change has been implemented successfully?

857. Are change requests logged and managed?

858. What are the duties of the change control team?

859. Will new change requests be acknowledged in a timely manner?

860. Where do changes come from?

861. How many lines of code must be changed to implement the change?

3.3 Change Log: Microsoft Dynamics 365 For Finance And Operations

862. Is the change backward compatible without limitations?

863. Is the submitted change a new change or a modification of a previously approved change?

864. How does this relate to the standards developed for specific business processes?

865. When was the request submitted?

866. Is the change request open, closed or pending?

867. Should a more thorough impact analysis be conducted?

868. When was the request approved?

869. Is this a mandatory replacement?

870. Do the described changes impact on the integrity or security of the system?

871. Is the requested change request a result of changes in other Microsoft Dynamics 365 For Finance And Operations project(s)?

872. Who initiated the change request?

873. Will the Microsoft Dynamics 365 For Finance And

Operations project fail if the change request is not executed?

874. How does this change affect the timeline of the schedule?

875. How does this change affect scope?

876. Does the suggested change request seem to represent a necessary enhancement to the product?

877. Is the change request within Microsoft Dynamics 365 For Finance And Operations project scope?

3.4 Decision Log: Microsoft Dynamics 365 For Finance And Operations

878. Does anything need to be adjusted?

879. Who will be given a copy of this document and where will it be kept?

880. Do strategies and tactics aimed at less than full control reduce the costs of management or simply shift the cost burden?

881. Adversarial environment. is your opponent open to a non-traditional workflow, or will it likely challenge anything you do?

882. It becomes critical to track and periodically revisit both operational effectiveness; Are you noticing all that you need to, and are you interpreting what you see effectively?

883. Is your opponent open to a non-traditional workflow, or will it likely challenge anything you do?

884. What was the rationale for the decision?

885. What alternatives/risks were considered?

886. How does provision of information, both in terms of content and presentation, influence acceptance of alternative strategies?

887. What makes you different or better than others

companies selling the same thing?

888. How effective is maintaining the log at facilitating organizational learning?

889. Meeting purpose; why does this team meet?

890. Decision-making process; how will the team make decisions?

891. What is the line where eDiscovery ends and document review begins?

892. What is your overall strategy for quality control / quality assurance procedures?

893. At what point in time does loss become unacceptable?

894. Who is the decisionmaker?

895. How do you know when you are achieving it?

896. How does an increasing emphasis on cost containment influence the strategies and tactics used?

897. With whom was the decision shared or considered?

3.5 Quality Audit: Microsoft Dynamics 365 For Finance And Operations

898. Is the continuing professional education of key personnel account fored in detail?

899. Does the supplier use a formal quality system?

900. How does your organization know that its risk management system is appropriately effective and constructive?

901. Have personnel cleanliness and health requirements been established?

902. How do staff know if they are doing a good job?

903. What is the collective experience of the team to be assigned to an audit?

904. Do the suppliers use a formal quality system?

905. Does the report read coherently?

906. How does your organization know that its staff entrance standards are appropriately effective and constructive and being implemented consistently?

907. How does your organization know that its Mission, Vision and Values Statements are appropriate and effectively guiding your organization?

908. Is there a written corporate quality policy?

909. How does the organization know that its system for maintaining and advancing the capabilities of its staff, particularly in relation to the Mission of the organization, is appropriately effective and constructive?

910. How does your organization know that its methods are appropriately effective and constructive?

911. Are all areas associated with the storage and reconditioning of devices clean, free of rubbish, adequately ventilated and in good repair?

912. Is your organizational structure established and each positions responsibility defined?

913. What are your supplier audits?

914. Does the suppliers quality system have a written procedure for corrective action when a defect occurs?

915. How does your organization know that its general support services planning and management systems are appropriately effective and constructive?

916. How does your organization know that its relationships with other relevant organizations are appropriately effective and constructive?

917. How does your organization know that its processes for managing severance are appropriately effective, constructive and fair?

3.6 Team Directory: Microsoft Dynamics 365 For Finance And Operations

918. Process decisions: do job conditions warrant additional actions to collect job information and document on-site activity?

919. When will you produce deliverables?

920. Who will report Microsoft Dynamics 365 For Finance And Operations project status to all stakeholders?

921. Is construction on schedule?

922. How does the team resolve conflicts and ensure tasks are completed?

923. Who is the Sponsor?

924. How will the team handle changes?

925. Who should receive information (all stakeholders)?

926. Have you decided when to celebrate the Microsoft Dynamics 365 For Finance And Operations projects completion date?

927. How will you accomplish and manage the objectives?

928. Who are the Team Members?

929. Who will talk to the customer?

930. What needs to be communicated?

931. Who will write the meeting minutes and distribute?

932. Process decisions: how well was task order work performed?

933. Where should the information be distributed?

934. Process decisions: is work progressing on schedule and per contract requirements?

935. Contract requirements complied with?

936. Does a Microsoft Dynamics 365 For Finance And Operations project team directory list all resources assigned to the Microsoft Dynamics 365 For Finance And Operations project?

937. Process decisions: are there any statutory or regulatory issues relevant to the timely execution of work?

3.7 Team Operating Agreement: Microsoft Dynamics 365 For Finance And Operations

938. Have you established procedures that team members can follow to work effectively together, such as a team operating agreement?

939. What went well?

940. What individual strengths does each team member bring to the group?

941. Methodologies: how will key team processes be implemented, such as training, research, work deliverable production, review and approval processes, knowledge management, and meeting procedures?

942. What is the number of cases currently teamed?

943. What administrative supports will be put in place to support the team and the teams supervisor?

944. Do you begin with a question to engage everyone?

945. Did you draft the meeting agenda?

946. Reimbursements: how will the team members be reimbursed for expenses and time commitments?

947. How will your group handle planned absences?

948. Are there more than two native languages represented by your team?

949. Does your team need access to all documents and information at all times?

950. Are there influences outside the team that may affect performance, and if so, have you identified and addressed them?

951. Must your team members rely on the expertise of other members to complete tasks?

952. Is compensation based on team and individual performance?

953. To whom do you deliver your services?

954. Do you record meetings for the already stated unable to attend?

955. Do you solicit member feedback about meetings and what would make them better?

956. Conflict resolution: how will disputes and other conflicts be mediated or resolved?

957. What are the boundaries (organizational or geographic) within which you operate?

3.8 Team Performance Assessment: Microsoft Dynamics 365 For Finance And Operations

958. If you are worried about method variance before you collect data, what sort of design elements might you include to reduce or eliminate the threat of method variance?

959. To what degree does the teams purpose constitute a broader, deeper aspiration than just accomplishing short-term goals?

960. To what degree does the teams work approach provide opportunity for members to engage in fact-based problem solving?

961. Lack of method variance in self-reported affect and perceptions at work: Reality or artifact?

962. What do you think is the most constructive thing that could be done now to resolve considerations and disputes about method variance?

963. What makes opportunities more or less obvious?

964. To what degree can team members frequently and easily communicate with one another?

965. To what degree do team members feel that the purpose of the team is important, if not exciting?

966. What are teams?

967. To what degree are fresh input and perspectives systematically caught and added (for example, through information and analysis, new members, and senior sponsors)?

968. How do you encourage members to learn from each other?

969. To what degree can team members meet frequently enough to accomplish the teams ends?

970. To what degree does the teams purpose contain themes that are particularly meaningful and memorable?

971. When a reviewer complains about method variance, what is the essence of the complaint?

972. To what degree is the team cognizant of small wins to be celebrated along the way?

973. To what degree do team members frequently explore the teams purpose and its implications?

974. How does Microsoft Dynamics 365 For Finance And Operations project termination impact Microsoft Dynamics 365 For Finance And Operations project team members?

975. To what degree will the team ensure that all members equitably share the work essential to the success of the team?

976. To what degree can team members vigorously define the teams purpose in considerations with

others who are not part of the functioning team?

977. Effects of crew composition on crew performance: Does the whole equal the sum of its parts?

3.9 Team Member Performance Assessment: Microsoft Dynamics 365 For Finance And Operations

978. What evidence supports your decision-making?

979. What are best practices for delivering and developing training evaluations to maximize the benefits of leveraging emerging technologies?

980. To what degree do team members articulate the teams work approach?

981. Are there any safeguards to prevent intentional or unintentional rating errors?

982. Is there reluctance to join a team?

983. How are performance measures and associated incentives developed?

984. Does platform-specific assessment information contribute to training placement or tailoring of instruction (e.g. aptitude-treatment interaction)?

985. Does adaptive training work?

986. Who they are?

987. What qualities does a successful Team leader possess?

988. Does the rater (supervisor) have the authority or

responsibility to tell an employee that the employees performance is unsatisfactory?

989. To what degree does the team possess adequate membership to achieve its ends?

990. What entity leads the process, selects a potential restructuring option and develops the plan?

991. Are any governance changes sufficient to impact achievement?

992. How will you identify your Team Leaders?

993. New skills/knowledge gained this year?

994. What is the role of the Reviewer?

3.10 Issue Log: Microsoft Dynamics 365 For Finance And Operations

995. Are you constantly rushing from meeting to meeting?

996. What effort will a change need?

997. Why multiple evaluators?

998. In classifying stakeholders, which approach to do so are you using?

999. How do you manage human resources?

1000. Who is the issue assigned to?

1001. What are the typical contents?

1002. Which team member will work with each stakeholder?

1003. How much time does it take to do it?

1004. What would have to change?

1005. Who have you worked with in past, similar initiatives?

1006. Do you have members of your team responsible for certain stakeholders?

1007. Are they needed?

1008. What is the impact on the risks?

1009. Is the issue log kept in a safe place?

4.0 Monitoring and Controlling Process Group: Microsoft Dynamics 365 For Finance And Operations

1010. Are there areas that need improvement?

1011. Did the Microsoft Dynamics 365 For Finance And Operations project team have the right skills?

1012. How well did the chosen processes fit the needs of the Microsoft Dynamics 365 For Finance And Operations project?

1013. How many potential communications channels exist on the Microsoft Dynamics 365 For Finance And Operations project?

1014. Is it what was agreed upon?

1015. Is there sufficient funding available for this?

1016. Who are the Microsoft Dynamics 365 For Finance And Operations project stakeholders?

1017. Key stakeholders to work with. How many potential communications channels exist on the Microsoft Dynamics 365 For Finance And Operations project?

1018. User: who wants the information and what are they interested in?

1019. Were sponsors and decision makers available

when needed outside regularly scheduled meetings?

1020. Just how important is your work to the overall success of the Microsoft Dynamics 365 For Finance And Operations project?

1021. Who needs to be involved in the planning?

1022. Based on your Microsoft Dynamics 365 For Finance And Operations project communication management plan, what worked well?

1023. What business situation is being addressed?

1024. Change, where should you look for problems?

1025. Propriety: who needs to be involved in the evaluation to be ethical?

1026. How many more potential communications channels were introduced by the discovery of the new stakeholders?

4.1 Project Performance Report: Microsoft Dynamics 365 For Finance And Operations

1027. To what degree do individual skills and abilities match task demands?

1028. To what degree does the teams work approach provide opportunity for members to engage in open interaction?

1029. To what degree can the cognitive capacity of individuals accommodate the flow of information?

1030. To what degree are the tasks requirements reflected in the flow and storage of information?

1031. To what degree can the team ensure that all members are individually and jointly accountable for the teams purpose, goals, approach, and work-products?

1032. To what degree does the information network provide individuals with the information they require?

1033. To what degree does the teams approach to its work allow for modification and improvement over time?

1034. To what degree are the demands of the task compatible with and converge with the mission and functions of the formal organization?

1035. To what degree do the structures of the formal organization motivate taskrelevant behavior and facilitate task completion?

1036. To what degree will team members, individually and collectively, commit time to help themselves and others learn and develop skills?

1037. What is the degree to which rules govern information exchange between individuals within your organization?

1038. To what degree will new and supplemental skills be introduced as the need is recognized?

1039. To what degree are the members clear on what they are individually responsible for and what they are jointly responsible for?

4.2 Variance Analysis: Microsoft Dynamics 365 For Finance And Operations

1040. Why are standard cost systems used?

1041. How does the use of a single conversion element (rather than the traditional labor and overhead elements) affect standard costing?

1042. Wbs elements contractually specified for reporting of status to your organization (lowest level only)?

1043. How does the monthly budget compare to the actual experience?

1044. What was the cause of the increase in costs?

1045. Who are responsible for the establishment of budgets and assignment of resources for overhead performance?

1046. The anticipated business volume?

1047. Is cost and schedule performance measurement done in a consistent, systematic manner?

1048. Is the market likely to continue to grow at this rate next year?

1049. Is the entire contract planned in time-phased control accounts to the extent practicable?

1050. Are the actual costs used for variance analysis reconcilable with data from the accounting system?

1051. What is the dollar amount of the fluctuation?

1052. What does a favorable labor efficiency variance mean?

1053. What does an unfavorable overhead volume variance mean?

1054. How do you identify potential or actual overruns and underruns?

1055. Does the contractors system provide unit or lot costs when applicable?

1056. Did an existing competitor change strategy?

1057. Are material costs reported within the same period as that in which BCWP is earned for that material?

4.3 Earned Value Status: Microsoft Dynamics 365 For Finance And Operations

1058. When is it going to finish?

1059. Where is evidence-based earned value in your organization reported?

1060. How much is it going to cost by the finish?

1061. Verification is a process of ensuring that the developed system satisfies the stakeholders agreements and specifications; Are you building the product right? What do you verify?

1062. How does this compare with other Microsoft Dynamics 365 For Finance And Operations projects?

1063. Earned value can be used in almost any Microsoft Dynamics 365 For Finance And Operations project situation and in almost any Microsoft Dynamics 365 For Finance And Operations project environment. it may be used on large Microsoft Dynamics 365 For Finance And Operations projects, medium sized Microsoft Dynamics 365 For Finance And Operations projects, tiny Microsoft Dynamics 365 For Finance And Operations projects (in cut-down form), complex and simple Microsoft Dynamics 365 For Finance And Operations projects and in any market sector. some people, of course, know all about earned value, they have used it for years - but perhaps not as effectively as they could have?

1064. What is the unit of forecast value?

1065. Validation is a process of ensuring that the developed system will actually achieve the stakeholders desired outcomes; Are you building the right product? What do you validate?

1066. Are you hitting your Microsoft Dynamics 365 For Finance And Operations projects targets?

1067. If earned value management (EVM) is so good in determining the true status of a Microsoft Dynamics 365 For Finance And Operations project and Microsoft Dynamics 365 For Finance And Operations project its completion, why is it that hardly any one uses it in information systems related Microsoft Dynamics 365 For Finance And Operations projects?

1068. Where are your problem areas?

4.4 Risk Audit: Microsoft Dynamics 365 For Finance And Operations

1069. Are procedures in place to ensure the security of staff and information and compliance with privacy legislation if applicable?

1070. Do the people have the right combinations of skills?

1071. What are the commonly used work arounds in high risk areas?

1072. What responsibilities for quality, errors, and outcomes have been delegated to staff (or others) without adequate oversight?

1073. When your organization is entering into a major contract, does it seek legal advice?

1074. Do you have position descriptions for all key paid and volunteer positions in your organization?

1075. Are all participants informed of safety issues?

1076. Are you aware of the industry standards that apply to your operations?

1077. What is the effect of globalisation; is business becoming too complex and can the auditor rely on auditing standards?

1078. If applicable; are compilers and code generators

available and suitable for the product to be built?

1079. Are tool mentors available?

1080. Is the auditor able to evaluate contradictory evidence in an unbiased manner?

1081. To what extent are auditors influenced by the business risk assessment in the audit process, and how can auditors create more effective mental models to more fully examine contradictory evidence?

1082. Is safety information provided to all involved?

1083. How effective are your risk controls?

1084. Is the customer willing to participate in reviews?

1085. What are the differences and similarities between strategic and operational risks in your organization?

1086. Has risk management been considered when planning an event?

1087. Does your organization have an up-to-date constitution?

4.5 Contractor Status Report: Microsoft Dynamics 365 For Finance And Operations

1088. How does the proposed individual meet each requirement?

1089. What was the budget or estimated cost for your organizations services?

1090. What process manages the contracts?

1091. What was the overall budget or estimated cost?

1092. How long have you been using the services?

1093. If applicable; describe your standard schedule for new software version releases. Are new software version releases included in the standard maintenance plan?

1094. Describe how often regular updates are made to the proposed solution. Are corresponding regular updates included in the standard maintenance plan?

1095. What is the average response time for answering a support call?

1096. What was the actual budget or estimated cost for your organizations services?

1097. Who can list a Microsoft Dynamics 365 For Finance And Operations project as organization experience, your organization or a previous employee of your organization?

1098. What are the minimum and optimal bandwidth requirements for the proposed solution?

1099. Are there contractual transfer concerns?

1100. How is risk transferred?

1101. What was the final actual cost?

4.6 Formal Acceptance: Microsoft Dynamics 365 For Finance And Operations

1102. How does your team plan to obtain formal acceptance on your Microsoft Dynamics 365 For Finance And Operations project?

1103. What lessons were learned about your Microsoft Dynamics 365 For Finance And Operations project management methodology?

1104. What is the Acceptance Management Process?

1105. Do you buy pre-configured systems or build your own configuration?

1106. General estimate of the costs and times to complete the Microsoft Dynamics 365 For Finance And Operations project?

1107. Was the Microsoft Dynamics 365 For Finance And Operations project goal achieved?

1108. Have all comments been addressed?

1109. Who would use it?

1110. Does it do what client said it would?

1111. Did the Microsoft Dynamics 365 For Finance And Operations project manager and team act in a professional and ethical manner?

1112. Who supplies data?

1113. Was business value realized?

1114. Was the Microsoft Dynamics 365 For Finance And Operations project work done on time, within budget, and according to specification?

1115. Was the sponsor/customer satisfied?

1116. Did the Microsoft Dynamics 365 For Finance And Operations project achieve its MOV?

1117. What function(s) does it fill or meet?

1118. Was the Microsoft Dynamics 365 For Finance And Operations project managed well?

1119. How well did the team follow the methodology?

1120. What can you do better next time?

1121. What was done right?

5.0 Closing Process Group: Microsoft Dynamics 365 For Finance And Operations

1122. If action is called for, what form should it take?

1123. What will you do to minimize the impact should a risk event occur?

1124. How will you do it?

1125. What can you do better next time, and what specific actions can you take to improve?

1126. Were risks identified and mitigated?

1127. What areas does the group agree are the biggest success on the Microsoft Dynamics 365 For Finance And Operations project?

1128. What level of risk does the proposed budget represent to the Microsoft Dynamics 365 For Finance And Operations project?

1129. What will you do?

1130. How will staff learn how to use the deliverables?

1131. How critical is the Microsoft Dynamics 365 For Finance And Operations project success to the success of your organization?

1132. Did the Microsoft Dynamics 365 For Finance

And Operations project management methodology work?

1133. Did you do things well?

1134. What could be done to improve the process?

1135. What areas were overlooked on this Microsoft Dynamics 365 For Finance And Operations project?

1136. What is the amount of funding and what Microsoft Dynamics 365 For Finance And Operations project phases are funded?

5.1 Procurement Audit: Microsoft Dynamics 365 For Finance And Operations

1137. Has your organization procedures in place to monitor the input of experts employed to assist the procurement function?

1138. Is the purchasing department facility laid out to facilitate interviews with salespersons?

1139. Were bids properly evaluated?

1140. When corresponding references were made, was a precise description of the performance not otherwise possible and were the already stated references accompanied by the words or equivalent?

1141. Was the dynamic purchasing system set up following the rules of open procedure?

1142. Is the performance of the procurement function/unit regularly evaluated?

1143. Are the responsibilities of the purchasing department clearly defined?

1144. Proper and complete records of transactions and events are maintained?

1145. Are contract changes after awarding properly justified and executed?

1146. Do all requests for materials, supplies, and services require supervisors authorization?

1147. Is the procurement process organized the most appropriate way taking into consideration the amount of procurement?

1148. How do you address the risk of fraud and corruption?

1149. Has an upper limit of cost been fixed?

1150. Does the procurement function/unit have the ability to negotiate with customers and suppliers?

1151. Were exclusion causes duly considered before the actual evaluation of tenders?

1152. Does the cash disbursement policy prohibit drawing checks to cash or bearer?

1153. Audits: when was your last independent public accountant (ipa) audit and what were the results?

1154. Did the contracting authority offer unrestricted and full electronic access to the contract documents and any supplementary documents (specifying the internet address in the notice)?

1155. Are checks disbursed by someone other than the individual who authorized payment?

1156. Has it been determined which shared services the procurement function/unit should be part of?

5.2 Contract Close-Out: Microsoft Dynamics 365 For Finance And Operations

1157. How does it work?

1158. Parties: Authorized?

1159. How is the contracting office notified of the automatic contract close-out?

1160. How/when used ?

1161. Have all acceptance criteria been met prior to final payment to contractors?

1162. Was the contract sufficiently clear so as not to result in numerous disputes and misunderstandings?

1163. Have all contract records been included in the Microsoft Dynamics 365 For Finance And Operations project archives?

1164. Have all contracts been completed?

1165. What is capture management?

1166. Change in knowledge?

1167. What happens to the recipient of services?

1168. Change in circumstances?

1169. Was the contract complete without requiring numerous changes and revisions?

1170. Has each contract been audited to verify acceptance and delivery?

1171. Are the signers the authorized officials?

1172. Why Outsource?

1173. Change in attitude or behavior?

1174. Parties: who is involved?

1175. Have all contracts been closed?

1176. Was the contract type appropriate?

5.3 Project or Phase Close-Out: Microsoft Dynamics 365 For Finance And Operations

1177. Who exerted influence that has positively affected or negatively impacted the Microsoft Dynamics 365 For Finance And Operations project?

1178. Does the lesson educate others to improve performance?

1179. What was learned?

1180. What process was planned for managing issues/ risks?

1181. What hierarchical authority does the stakeholder have in your organization?

1182. What security considerations needed to be addressed during the procurement life cycle?

1183. What information did each stakeholder need to contribute to the Microsoft Dynamics 365 For Finance And Operations projects success?

1184. What benefits or impacts does the stakeholder group expect to obtain as a result of the Microsoft Dynamics 365 For Finance And Operations project?

1185. Was the schedule met?

1186. In addition to assessing whether the Microsoft

Dynamics 365 For Finance And Operations project was successful, it is equally critical to analyze why it was or was not fully successful. Are you including this?

1187. Were cost budgets met?

1188. Were the outcomes different from the already stated planned?

1189. What is the information level of detail required for each stakeholder?

1190. Was the user/client satisfied with the end product?

1191. Who controlled the resources for the Microsoft Dynamics 365 For Finance And Operations project?

1192. Planned completion date?

1193. Who are the Microsoft Dynamics 365 For Finance And Operations project stakeholders and what are roles and involvement?

5.4 Lessons Learned: Microsoft Dynamics 365 For Finance And Operations

1194. Was the Microsoft Dynamics 365 For Finance And Operations project manager sufficiently experienced, skilled, trained, supported?

1195. What is the value of the deliverable?

1196. How useful was your testing?

1197. What was the single greatest success and the single greatest shortcoming or challenge from the Microsoft Dynamics 365 For Finance And Operations projects perspective?

1198. Was there a Microsoft Dynamics 365 For Finance And Operations project Definition document. Was there a Microsoft Dynamics 365 For Finance And Operations project Plan. Were they used during the Microsoft Dynamics 365 For Finance And Operations project?

1199. What were the major enablers to a quick response?

1200. Why does your organization need a lessons learned (LL) capability?

1201. Was the necessary hardware, software, accommodation etc available?

1202. How effective was Microsoft Dynamics 365 For Finance And Operations project Team member training?

1203. How mature are the observations?

1204. Does the lesson describe a function that would be done differently the next time?

1205. How often did you violate the rules?

1206. How comprehensive was integration testing?

1207. How clear were you on your role in the Microsoft Dynamics 365 For Finance And Operations project?

1208. How well does the product or service the Microsoft Dynamics 365 For Finance And Operations project produced meet your needs?

1209. What is the quality and content of communication?

1210. How effectively and consistently was sponsorship for the Microsoft Dynamics 365 For Finance And Operations project conveyed?

1211. Whom to share Lessons Learned Information with?

1212. Are you in full regulatory compliance?

1213. What worked well or did not work well, either for this Microsoft Dynamics 365 For Finance And Operations project or for the Microsoft Dynamics 365

For Finance And Operations project team?

Index

Made in United States
Orlando, FL
15 September 2022

22439070R00193